Deadline Busting

Deadline Busting

✦

How to be a Star Performer in Your Organization

Jeffrey Ford, Ph.D.
Laurie Ford, Ph.D.

iUniverse, Inc.
New York Lincoln Shanghai

Deadline Busting
How to be a Star Performer in Your Organization

iUniverse books may be ordered through booksellers or by contacting:

iUniverse
2021 Pine Lake Road, Suite 100
Lincoln, NE 68512
www.iuniverse.com
1-800-Authors (1-800-288-4677)

ISBN-13: 978-0-595-33906-8 (pbk)
ISBN-13: 978-0-595-67031-4 (cloth)
ISBN-13: 978-0-595-78692-3 (ebk)
ISBN-10: 0-595-33906-9 (pbk)
ISBN-10: 0-595-67031-8 (cloth)
ISBN-10: 0-595-78692-8 (ebk)

Printed in the United States of America

Contents

Acknowledgements

This material comes from the work we've done with thousands of managers, clients and students. We are grateful for the problems they have posed to us, for their commitment to finding ways to get things done, and for allowing us into their work lives. Without these, this book would not have been possible.

Although we are solely responsible for the content of this book, many people have contributed ideas, suggestions, and recommendations. Ney Arias, Bill Ayscue, Brad Gibson, Beth Keehn, Jonathan Rush, Stephanie Sanders and Shawn Stevenson participated in a special ten week course, not only "test driving" the entire collection of tips in their jobs, but also discussing and exploring the underlying issues involved in meeting deadlines. We are grateful for their contribution and their hard work. We learned from them.

Brian Stuhlmuller, Andrea DiCarlo, Angelo D'Amelio, Susan Alexander, and Sarah McKee listened to our ideas as they were being developed and gave insightful comments as well as ongoing encouragement. This book is better because of their contribution.

We have also benefited from the extensive writings in management theory, sociology, psychology and communication theory as well as countless professional and trade books. The educational programs of Landmark Education and Mission Control Productivity, Inc. have also been instrumental in shaping our thinking, and we thank them for the difference they have made for us.

Preface

Tom Cruise. Julia Roberts. Russell Crowe. What do these three people have in common? Each is a movie star. Movie-goers use the term "star" to refer to anyone who plays a lead role. Each of these three people performs in lead roles, but they are also stars for another reason. They deliver at the box office, and they do it consistently.

It's said that adding Tom Cruise to the lead role of a movie can be worth an additional $15 million at the box office. Not only is he a good actor, but he has proven himself to be a reliable draw at the box office. Small wonder he's in such demand and receives so many offers.

How many of us would love to be a star performer like Tom Cruise, Julia Roberts, or Russell Crowe—or any of a number of others? Unfortunately, we can't help you with movie offers, but we can help you become a star performer in your own organization.

Every organization has stars. In fact, every organization depends on stars for their financial, operational and cultural success. Who are they? Organizational stars are the people that managers call "go-to people." They are the people managers go to when they must get something done. Organizational stars, under virtually any circumstance, can be counted on to make things happen. They will deliver what is wanted, where it is wanted and when it is wanted to the people who want it. Like the Tom Cruises of the world, organizational stars deliver.

We call these people Deadline Busters: people who can meet, and beat, a deadline, a target or a goal. Perhaps you know some people like this. In fact, maybe you are one of them. Deadline Busters will get something done, no matter what the constraints. You can "bet the ranch" they will deliver the results you need, when and where you need them.

Unlike movie stars, star performers in organizations are not necessarily celebrities. Some Deadline Busters are not well known, even to their peers. Their managers, of course, know who they are and have come to rely on them. Maybe you know them as "trouble shooters", or as "go-to people," or as people who break the usual performance curves.

Deadline Busters tend to get more recognition than others. They also tend to get more interesting job assignments, bigger raises, and more promotions. And they get consistently high performance evaluations. Because of their reputation, they are sometimes asked to participate in more important meetings, or to spend more time with the higher ups. They are go-getters in the sense that they are challenged by the "game" of meeting and beating a deadline or a target.

YOU CAN BE A STAR

We have studied and collaborated with organizational star performers for years, and have learned something very interesting: people aren't born stars. Organization stars are not born, they are created. It takes a combination of attitude and action, which can be learned if you're willing to break some old habits and learn some new ones. People can learn to be stars. You can be a star—a Deadline Buster—if you want to be.

We've learned also that the difference between star performers and good performers is not a huge leap. If you are already a good performer, only one or two new things could make a difference to have you be a star Deadline Buster. Some of the practices in this book can move a good performer into the Deadline Buster category. How can you tell if you're ready? Ask yourself a few questions.

Should I read this book? If you're sitting through your work days counting the hours until retirement (or vacation, or Friday), this book won't be a useful tool for you. But you should read it if you want or need to be more in charge in your work life. Or—

- If you want better performance reviews, better job assignments and bigger raises,
- If you've just been promoted and now have more deadlines requiring you to improve your on-time performance,
- If you've just been promoted and you are now managing other people,
- If you just want to start delivering everything you are supposed to deliver, and do it on time and under budget—in other words, you're ready to be successful.

If you want to be a star, give yourself some time with this book.

Okay, but what is "Deadline Busting"? Deadline Busting is being able to reliably do what you said you would do, deliver the results to the people who expect them, and do it all on time. It's being responsible for your deadlines.

But what if I don't have many deadlines? If you have a "To Do" list, you have deadlines. If you ever say you'll do something for someone, you have a deadline. Even if your deadline seems to be a vague "someday" rather than a specific due date, you still have someone expecting to get something from you. Your choice is whether to be a victim of scarce resources, disorganization, and poor communications, or to beat the game and be a Deadline Buster.

Everyone misses deadlines. Why should I care if I miss them? Short answer: because your reputation at work depends on it. You'll discover in **Chapter 1—"There Are No Loopholes In Yes,"** that people in your workplace make judgments about you, and about what kind of performer you are, based on your ability to deliver the goods. These judgments have an effect on your evaluations, promotions and pay raises, and even the kind of job assignments you'll get or the new opportunities that will be opened for you. Deadline Busting is a set of well-tested and proven ideas that will give you ways to improve your performance. You'll develop a new ability to do what you say you will do. The result: you'll be more effective. Your reputation will start to shine, because people notice on-time results and reliable performance. Deadline Busters are an organization's "go-to" people.

Whoa…it sounds as if I'll just get more work! I can't get everything done that I already have in front of me. It's true, you just might get more work to do. In today's working world, everyone is getting more and more to do, regardless of how effective he or she is. You also might start to get different kinds of work, more interesting and varied. But we promise you'll have less stress about it. We also promise you'll have a greater sense of accomplishment out of it. And we promise you'll be in a better position to get things done whenever you say yes to them. You'll see in **Chapter 2—Saying Yes but Doing No**, that people say they'll do lots of things they never do, and have a million reasons for not doing them. But once you've practiced even a few Deadline Busting ideas, you'll notice that when you say yes, it means something. Your world will begin to take notice, and things will start to move your way.

Well, I could get more things done on time if I could change some of the people I work with. Am I going to learn how to do that? No, not directly. Deadline Busting is designed for <u>you</u>. In **Chapter 3—Getting Beyond Reasons,** you'll see your own unique way of operating at work. You'll also find it's not hard to make a few small changes that have a big effect on people around you. In fact, the most powerful way to improve your performance reputation is by working on <u>you</u>. Only you can do it. Don't bother changing other people—just work on yourself first. It's easier and more interesting anyway.

Is there some special method or process I have to learn and apply? No, but you'll see in **Chapter 4—The Tips,** eighty-five tips on how to improve your performance on deadlines. You'll learn about when and how to say yes. You'll learn how to manage your business relationships in new ways. And you'll learn about saying no. These tips come from the experiences of thousands of managers. You'll see which will be the most useful to you, in your situation. Some will be immediately useful, others will be of value at a later time, and some may never be relevant for you in your current job or type of business. You will decide what to use and what to ignore. And because they're in the form of tips, instead of a method or a series of steps, you can choose the order you want to test them in your job. In **Chapter 5—What's Next?** you'll get ideas for how to implement the tips. *One* guarantee: practicing even a few of these tips will make a difference in your ability to be reliable and meet deadlines.

Is this some form of time management? No, Deadline Busting is not time management. If you want good time management, try a program like David Allen's "Getting Things Done," or a personal productivity program like those offered by Mission Control Productivity Inc. Deadline Busting is about your ability to manage the communications around your work, and the processes of overseeing, coordinating, and doing the work itself, so you can meet and beat deadlines and do it consistently.

Many people say they have no control in their jobs, or they've lost control of their life at work. People say they feel rushed, stressed and overwhelmed with everything they have to do. And, making it worse, people are bothered about the things they've promised that are not getting done, are overdue, or aren't getting done well. Deadline Busting is about putting you in the driver's seat of your work life.

Fundamentally, Deadline Busting is about telling the truth about deadlines. What's the real reason things don't get done on time? What can change that? When you begin to practice some of the tips, you'll start to gain more control over your work, and take responsibility for your work in a new and more powerful way. It's not difficult. And it will set you apart: you will be trusted to do what you say. Your word will count.

1

There Are No Loopholes in Yes

"Would some power give us the gift to see ourselves as others see us.
It would from many a blunder free us."

—Robert Burns, Scottish Poet

FedEx has an advertisement showing a woman, walking down a busy city street carrying a box. Prominently displayed on the box is the word FedEx. Under the woman's picture are the following words:

Ours isn't the only name on the box. Amy's reputation is on the line. When her client asks if the contracts will arrive in the morning, Amy says "yes." Brave Amy, delving into the world of "yes." "Yes" raises the stakes. "Yes" comes with responsibility. There are no loopholes in "yes." Is Amy worried? No. Relax, its FedEx.

Perhaps you are familiar with this ad, or one like it, that talks about having a good reputation. Most of the well-known delivery services make such claims. FedEx, UPS, and other delivery companies sell more than delivery services. They sell their reputation: a reputation for delivering on time, every time. This reputation is the main reason so many people trust these companies with their packages; they promise to do what they say.

The important point is that it's not their reputation alone they are selling. They are also selling their promise to improve your reputation. They are, in effect, saying, "Our reputation is so good, that if you use us, your reputation will also be good. So, go ahead and say yes. With our reputation, you have nothing to worry about."

In the delivery business, there are no loopholes when you say yes. You either deliver or you don't, period. As Yoda, the Jedi master in Star Wars, told Luke Skywalker, "Do, or do not. There is no try." "I tried" is a loophole, and there are no loopholes here. You must deliver and you must deliver consistently, be reliable, and do what you say you will do. Saying "yes" is a promise you have to keep, or it kills your reputation.

EVERYONE IS IN THE DELIVERY BUSINESS

So why are we telling you about FedEx, UPS and the delivery business? Because if you work in an organization, any organization, you are in the delivery business. That is true regardless of your position in that organization. Whatever your job is, you are in the delivery business. If you have a job, you deliver. No delivery, no job.

That means whether you work for General Electric, Nationwide Insurance, or the U.S. Marines, you are in the delivery business. Whether you are a CEO, a vice president, a project manager or a supervisor, you are in the delivery business. Whether you are a fund raiser, a bookkeeper, or a secretary you are in the delivery business. What you deliver, and to whom, will be different depending on the organization and your position within that organization. But you are still in the delivery business.

Whenever someone asks you to do something for them and you say yes, you have promised to make a delivery at some time in the future. One way people ask you to deliver is by writing it into your job description. That means you've already said yes to a whole bunch of things before you even come to work each day. Whether explicit or implied, you have made a promise. Now you have to do something to keep from breaking it. You have to deliver.

You might need to deliver new software to clients, a report to your boss, or an expense report to Harriet in Accounting. You might need to deliver a performance review to an employee, a project plan to your team or a capital request to the CFO. Even responses to emails and phone calls, participation at meetings, and making requests or promises to peers are deliveries you might need to make in order to keep your promises to deliver. You can't escape the fact that whatever your job, whatever your position, you need to deliver things to others. Whether you deliver physical objects, services, information, or communications, you are in the delivery business.

Of course, there is more to the delivery business than making the delivery. There is all the work that goes on before the delivery. You may have to develop, assemble or test some things in order to produce whatever is to be delivered. A report to your boss, for example, requires getting the necessary information from other people, sorting and analyzing it, then organizing and preparing the final product. The report is what you deliver, but work is involved in producing it too.

So, you not only deliver, you probably also gather, sort and assemble materials and ideas in order to make the delivery as promised. You know that if any of these preliminary tasks doesn't get done, your delivery will be at risk. But that doesn't alter the fact that you are still, first and foremost, in the delivery business. In fact, the most visible aspect of your job is the delivery. People don't see all the work behind the scenes, but they do know whether or not the delivery happened.

When FedEx or UPS is late with a delivery, we don't know all the things they probably did in their attempt to get it delivered on time. We only know that it's late. Imagine: maybe planes broke down, pilots got sick, weather closed airports, delivery trucks had accidents, etc. But none of this matters to us if the package arrives damaged or late. Damaged is damaged and late is late.

THEY DON'T CARE

People don't care why a delivery was late or damaged, only that it was. This might seem harsh or even unfair, but think about a time when you were counting on a delivery and you didn't get it. Maybe it was a delivery you needed in order to keep your promise to someone else—an *important* someone else. Got one in mind? OK, were you upset about not getting the delivery? Angry? Worried? Did you care about their reasons why you didn't get it?

> A dad, taking his son to his Little League ball game, stopped at a pizza place and ordered a pizza. The order went in at 5:05 o'clock, and he was told it would be ready in about ten minutes. After waiting twenty minutes, the Dad inquired into the status of his pizza. The clerk asked the cooks for the pizza and was told, "We can't find it." The Dad asked to see the manager.
>
> When the manager arrived, the Dad complained, "I have been waiting for my pizza and now they tell me they can't find it. Can you tell me where it is?"
>
> The manager answered, "The person who took your order put it into the computer, and shouldn't have. The computer isn't working right. So now we have to take all the orders manually and he didn't know that. We weren't prepared for this. It's just a real mess."
>
> The Dad, somewhat upset at this point, replied, "I don't care why it's not ready. That's your problem. My problem is getting my son his dinner before his game. Can you tell me how much longer before we get our pizza?"

The pizza store manager forgot he was in the delivery business. The customer didn't want to know <u>why</u> the manager's system didn't work, only <u>when</u> the pizza would arrive. From the customer's standpoint, understanding why the pizza is late doesn't change anything. The pizza is still late.

What's worse is that the Dad is forming an opinion about the pizza place. The manager should be glad this customer is not writing his job performance evaluation: "Late service, poor communication with team, unresponsive to customer concerns."

Who writes your job performance evaluation? Maybe you are evaluated on whether you show initiative, demonstrate leadership, or meet deadlines. Whatever it is, you can be sure it involves delivering something to someone. Your knowledge of what you are supposed to deliver, the requirements and deadlines for the delivery, and the consistency with which you keep your delivery promises will determine your reputation. The person waiting for your delivery does not care about your reasons for lateness or all the problems you are dealing with right now. They just want their pizza.

EVERYONE HAS ONE

Everyone has a rep. Some people have great reputations: Tiger Woods, Michael Jordan, and Nelson Mandela. Other people are notorious, which means they have bad reps: Osama Bin Laden, Saddam Hussein and William Bundy, the serial killer. In your organization, who has a reputation for being smart? Responsible? Fun? Gossipy? Lazy? Dumb? We bet you know some of these people.

A reputation is a form of public identity. It is the way people are known, a label or a kind of shorthand that describes a pattern of conduct or performance. Often we don't know much about our own reputation, because it is created and spoken by other people. It also doesn't matter if you like, or agree with, your label. Your reputation is what other people say about you—your behavior, your attitude, and your performance.

Another way to think of your rep is like it's a report card or a grade that other people have given you. It's their summary impression of your performance based on what they have seen and heard you do and say, along with what others have said about you. When people's impression is that you are a high achiever, or honest, or responsible, it gives you a "good reputation" that helps them trust you. If people's impression is that you make excuses, undermine colleagues or avoid work, it gives you a poor reputation that causes them to be cautious about working with you. You probably know people who have some of these reputations:

- "hard worker"
- "good colleague"
- "teacher's pet"
- "tough, but fair"
- "not good with numbers"
- "highly emotional"
- "good listener"
- "real producer"
- "can't be counted on when it matters"

Each of these reputations sticks to people like a name tag, and tells us something about them. It also tells us what we might expect from them in the future. Although reputations are based on peoples' impressions from the past, they are used as indicators of future performance. Most people assume that what you did in the past is a pretty good predictor of what you will do in the future in a similar situation. It might not be fair that they do that, but they do.

Reputations help people answer the questions we all ask about our co-workers, bosses and other people in our work environment. We want to know: "What is she like?" "What can I expect from him?" and "Can I count on her to do that?" Peoples' reputations give us the bottom line about them. Each of us has one. Do you know yours?

SOME ARE FRAGILE, OTHERS ARE STICKY

Some reputations are fragile. The old adage that "One bad apple spoils the whole bunch" also applies to a good reputation. A good reputation may have been arduously constructed and painstakingly maintained, even taking a lifetime to build. But it can take only a single incident to destroy it. Martha Stewart's reputation as an honest and successful businesswoman took years of very hard work to build, and was unalterably damaged by her conviction for obstructing justice and lying to investigators about insider trading. Speculation is that it will take years for her to restore her reputation, if it can be done at all.

Other reputations, particularly of the "loser" or "failure" variety, appear to be much stickier. They have more staying power, even in the face of positive news. Phil Mickelson had a reputation of being the best golfer to never win a major championship. He was said to be a highly talented and accomplished failure, even though he was twice a runner-up at the U.S. Open, had a second-place finish at the PGA Championship, and had four third-place showings at the Masters.

But close is not enough: Phil's record was 0-42 in the majors, and so he had a reputation as a talented failure. Then he won the 2004 Masters golf tournament in Augusta, Georgia. When he made a twenty-foot putt on the last hole of the Masters to beat Ernie Els, Phil Mickelson apparently erased a reputation that had dogged him over the past ten years. So, it changed his reputation, right?

Maybe not. The pundits quickly began asking whether Phil had gotten better or whether his victory was simply a matter of having been so close so many times that he was bound to win one by chance. Maybe Phil got lucky.

Performance that is contrary to a reputation causes us to question our judgment, or to lose confidence or trust in ourselves or others. We wonder, question, and doubt. We wonder if we were wrong about people, or if things have changed after all. Martha Stewart may never regain her good name, and Phil Mickelson may never shake the loser image until he wins more major championships. The ease with which good reputations can plummet, and poor reputations persist, even in the face of contrary performance, is also true of reputations in the workplace.

Your reputation is the way people know you, and it determines whether people respect you, trust you, or believe in you. It decides the way people will treat you. Quite simply, reputations matter. If you want a good reputation, it takes work, not only to create it, but also to maintain it, and to defend it if it is threatened.

YOU CAN MAKE A REP FOR YOURSELF

Before going on, try this exercise. Think of some task at work that has to be done right. Who would you give it to? Why? Who would you not give it to? Why not? What you know about those two people is what we call their reputation. You use reputations to help you make decisions: who to hire, or fire; who to give an assignment to, or bypass; who to promote, or keep on the sidelines.

Companies and individuals work hard to create and maintain reputations that will bring them the benefits they want. They call it marketing, public relations, customer service or a thousand other names, but it all boils down to one idea: reputation-building.

Consider this example: Imagine that you plan a special romantic dinner for two. You want to go to someplace you have never been before, and you want it to be memorable. How will you choose where to go? Maybe by reading restaurant reviews, talking to friends or even looking at the number of cars in the parking lot. You may also have seen media advertisements, heard promotions or received coupons. The point is, all those places have tried their best to create a good reputation that will encourage you to give them your business. They are working hard to build a good reputation because they want to be successful.

Every individual in every workplace has the same opportunity: You can try to be successful, to move ahead, get a promotion or a raise, or get a good reference for a future employer, a better job or a more promising career. You will do it the same way businesses do it, by building a good reputation for yourself as a valued performer in your workplace.

You, like the restaurant, have a reputation that is passed around by word of mouth, by your resume, and by evaluations of your job performance. All these contribute to your reputation, and tell people what to expect of you. When your name comes up for an assignment, people determine whether you fit, or are right for the job. Every manager knows who their go-to people are when they need to get crucial projects done. If you, like the restaurant owners, want to get the benefits of success, you'll want to work on making a better and better name for yourself.

Reputation-building takes time and attention, but it is the single best investment you can make in yourself and your work life. The benefits go beyond having more interesting and worthwhile job assignments. You will receive better performance reviews, raises and promotions. You will have a solid work record, more credibility for the decisions you make, and people will want to work with you and support your projects and programs.

Bottom line: you will be more successful. This is the pathway to leadership. Reputations are a product of deliberate, intentional actions as well as accidents, so changing a reputation takes work. But some reputations are worth the challenge to create, improve, and maintain.

DEADLINE BUSTER—A REPUTATION WORTH HAVING

Some reputations are worth having. For example, it's good to be known as a valuable asset to your organization. Other reputations don't matter so much. The fact that you can drink beer through your nose probably won't increase your income or happiness beyond the neighborhood tavern.

One reputation worth having is a reputation for being a "Deadline Buster". This is a person who has a pattern of behavior and performance that is unique in organizations; he or she can be counted on to consistently meet and beat deadlines. Now, before you say, "But I don't have any deadlines, so this doesn't apply to me," answer one question. Do you have a "to do" list? Is there anything on the list that you are doing for someone else? If so, you have a deadline. It might not be a specific one with a solid due date, but you have a deadline because at some point that person is going to expect something from you. We have never encountered anyone in any organization who does not have deadlines.

Deadline Busters deliver at, or above, the levels expected of them. But they don't just get things done on time. They also get them done right, meaning complete, accurate and with quality. As a result, these people have a reputation for consistently high and reliable performance in the face of time constraints. Because they deliver what they say they will deliver, they are credible.

This is a good kind of reputation to have in the workplace. Not everyone can be a good organizer, or a good people-person, or a good detail-person. But everyone can become credible. You can improve your delivery to satisfy your promises by paying more attention to what you promise. Deadline Busters are willing to tell the truth about what they will deliver, and when. Their goal? To deliver on, or before, the deadline.

Why bother doing that? You shouldn't bother—unless you want a reputation for being someone who is count-on-able, reliable, who gets things done, or is a go-to person when things need to be done. If you're thinking, "But then I'd just get more work to do," then we must admit: it might be true. But you'll also get more interesting work to do. And you'll get the respect of the people who pay you, promote you, and care about the success of your organization. You'll also get that sweet taste of pride you get from busting deadlines, a rare and delicious accomplishment. Deadline Busting is about building and maintaining a reputation for exemplary performance in the race with time.

Regardless of your current reputation, it is possible to improve your reputation for credibility and reliable performance. It doesn't matter if you work by yourself or as part of a team. A survey of executives found that being a team player means meeting deadlines.[1] According to these executives, a reputation as a team player depends on the extent to which someone is a deadline buster.

Deadline Busting is not about perfection. Everyone, even deadline busters, sometimes misses a deadline. We're talking about altering the way you perform in the face of deadlines, so you become more consistent in your time-based performance.

Being a deadline buster is built on the premises we've established so far in this chapter:

1. If you have a job, you are in the delivery business. You have results and communications you're responsible for delivering to others.

2. If you are in the delivery business, all that matters is whether you keep your promises about those deliveries. Excuses don't count.

3. If you live and work around other human beings, you have a reputation that tells them whether or not you're reliable and credible with delivery.

4. You can affect your reputation for being credible by practice by saying what you'll deliver and delivering what you say.

5. If you do this, you will be extraordinary in your workplace and you'll get some major benefits out of it, including people's trust and confidence, better jobs, and more money.

Deadline Busting is about building your reputation for consistently meeting and beating deadlines. It's about developing the habits and practices that allow you to do what you say. Ultimately, it's about controlling your own success at work.

---

1.   "Reality Check", Haidee E. Allerton, <u>Training and Development</u>, September 1997, Vol. 51, Issue 9, p. 9.

2

Saying Yes, but Doing No

Have you ever had an assignment that <u>had</u> to be done by a particular date? Something critical, like completing the installation of a new computer system that was going live the next day. Or finishing a report for the chairman of the board to deliver at the annual board meeting that night. Or arranging for tonight's anniversary dinner party at your city's most exclusive restaurant. Whatever it was, it had to happen by the due date. There would be no tomorrow, next day or later.

Now add some complexity to that. What if you couldn't complete the assignment by yourself? What if you needed other people to do certain things for you? And what if the parts you needed to entrust to other people are also critical—things that had to be done right, and done on time, or you would miss the deadline?

Then, let's say you found the right person to do one of the key tasks, and that person said yes. When you saw her during that day and reminded her, she said, "Yes it will be done. Stop worrying." So you kept doing everything on your end to make sure the whole thing turned out well, confident that the other person would do what she said.

You know the punch line. She did not do what she said she would do. After saying yes, after all the assurances, she didn't do it. And as a result, your project was full of last-minute emergencies and problems and delays, all because somebody else dropped the ball. Sure, the person who blew it may have felt bad about it, and maybe she apologized, and maybe even gave a good explanation for why the task didn't get done. But all that didn't matter much, because you had a serious problem on your hands.

If this has happened to you, then you know what it means to work with someone who is "saying yes but doing no." You have experienced the "kiss of yes."[1] If you haven't had this experience, we're glad to hear it. But you should know that

---

1.   <u>The Reengineering Revolution: A Handbook</u>. Michael Hammer and Steven A. Stanton. Harper Business, 1995.

saying yes but doing no is common in the world of work. In fact, studies have shown that on-time delivery in most workplaces is only forty to eighty per cent.[2] It is very common for people to say when they will have something done, then deliver much later than promised, if at all.

THERE ARE REASONS

Saying yes but doing no is a kind of organizational sabotage. If I tell you, "No, I can't do it," or, "No, I won't do it," you might be unhappy with me, but at least you can make other arrangements to get your work done. A good, clean no is direct and straight, and you still have other opportunities to make things work out. But when I say yes and do no, I have misled you. Not only do you not get what you expected, you also don't get a chance to make other arrangements, which means you have a much more critical problem than if I had been straight with you in the first place. Your results are damaged or trashed, you've lost confidence and trust in me, and there is now added strain in the workplace that wasn't there before.

Given these high costs of saying yes but doing no, why does it keep happening? Why do people do no, even after saying yes? Why, even when we say yes with complete sincerity and every intention of doing the task, do we sometimes still do no?

Reason 1. I was too optimistic.

Most people are optimistic most of the time. We tend to exaggerate our own talents, believing we are above average in our abilities. A study of a million students conducted by the College Boards in the 1970s found that when asked to rate themselves in comparison to their peers, sixty per cent rated themselves in the top ten per cent! And twenty-five per cent rated themselves in the top one per cent![3] This study was investigating how well people thought they got along with others, but our fundamental optimism operates in many areas of our lives. Most people overestimate their ability to get things done and their ability to overcome problems.

---

2. "Why do we miss delivery dates?", K. Cyrus Hadavi, <u>Industrial Management</u>, Sept-Oct, 1996, pp. 1-4.
3. "Delusions of Success: How Optimism Undermines Executives' Decisions", Dan Lovallo and Daniel Kahneman, <u>Harvard Business Review</u>, July 2003, pp. 56-63.

This optimism contributes to what psychologists call the planning fallacy. This is the human tendency to make optimistic estimates of how long it will take to complete a task even when we've done similar tasks that took much longer than we thought they would. Not only do people overestimate their ability, they also underestimate the time required to complete the job. In the grip of the planning fallacy, people make decisions based on delusional optimism.[4]

To compound the optimism problem, people either ignore or discount important information about specific aspects of the task they are saying yes to, and don't recognize red flags indicating it will take longer or be more difficult this time. Potential problems, breakdowns or difficulties are dismissed as not applicable, as if to say, "That won't happen here."

As a result, people overestimate the probability of success while overlooking the potential for mistakes. They miscalculate the time and resources required to get the job done. Instead of a clear and rational consideration of the job in front of them, they have a distorted and unrealistically optimistic view.

One victim of optimism was a new consultant who asked an experienced colleague how much time she should estimate for a project she was bidding. The consultant said the project involved five interviews, analysis of the interview data, report preparation and presentation of recommendations. All together, the consultant estimated it should take about twenty hours. But her colleague said her estimate was low, and that she should triple it to sixty hours, or at least double it to forty hours. The experienced colleague knew there would be much more involved than those bare-boned tasks. The consultant, not believing it could take that much time, submitted the project bid for thirty hours. Several weeks later, she confessed, "I should have listened to you. I told them it would take thirty hours, and it ended up taking me more than fifty."

With an optimistic view, people believe they can-do, whether or not they have investigated the details. So we say yes, relying on our inflated opinion of ourselves and our tendency to ignore problem signals. Unfortunately, once we get into the work, we run into reality. The result? We end up doing no, and the promised work is not done by the deadline.

Reason 2. I procrastinated.

The most common reason for doing no is procrastination. This is the tendency to put off doing the work. Maybe you get started, then get interrupted and forget

---

4.   Ibid.

how much is left to be done. Maybe you just put the job in a stack and make a mental note to get to it later. But, by the time you do get back to it there is not enough time left to do it, or to do it right.

One demonstration of procrastination is called the deadline effect. This is the tendency to wait until half the time before the deadline has expired before we start the work. If we have a due date one month away, we are most likely to get started only after two weeks have already passed. Why? Because for the first two weeks, we feel there is plenty of time left. Only when the deadline is more real and looming do we get going. Once the midpoint to the deadline has been reached, we get to work. The closer the deadline, the longer and harder we work.

The deadline effect is a result of procrastination. It causes us increased stress and pressure as a deadline draws near. It gives us the hurry and panic we often find as a due date approaches. At that time, some people become seriously anxious; others are easily irritated, and almost everyone complains, "I have too much to do in too little time". This is the deadline effect at work.

As a procrastinator, I say yes because I think I have plenty of time to get things done, but end up doing no because I start late and run out of time. Procrastinators rely on getting things done at the last minute. Extending the due date will not cure a procrastinator, because the length of time given to do the work is not the problem. The problem is the late start.

Reason 3. I didn't plan and schedule my work.

Every task has certain timing attributes associated with it. Some parts of a task will need to be done in a particular order, and other parts are not time-dependent. Some parts of the task can be done at the same time, while others must be done in a sequence.

But here's the rule of gravity in the world of work: no matter what the timing attributes are, everything will require some period of time in which to do it. It might be a task that takes only a short period of time, a few minutes or a few hours. A more complicated job might take a longer period of time—several hours, or several time periods over many days, weeks or months. Whether the task will take one short period of time, or require multiple longer periods of time spread out over months, we know for sure that if the job is to be done, it will require one or more specific periods of time.

People miss deadlines because they do not think through the actual periods of time that will be required to do the job. The sequential parts of the job, the variable parts of the job, and the routine parts of the job all have to happen in time. If the task doesn't happen in time, it doesn't happen at all.

People have a tendency to do things on the fly, to improvise as they go, and to figure things out when they get to them. Most people usually give little or no practical consideration to the flow of events and actions that must occur to get the work done. This is partly because they don't feel they have the time to plan. Or they think that planning is a waste of time because most plans change at least once in the course of a job. But without planning, issues of timing and coordination are overlooked, and some things are forgotten until the last minute. The result is that people don't plan their work in a way it can be scheduled effectively.

Even though people know things take time to do, they don't set aside periods of time in their personal schedules to do them. In fact, most personal calendars are full of blank space, which looks suspiciously like "free time" to the naïve observer. In fact, those blank spaces are imagined to accept a host of tasks that people think might fit in that time. But nothing is written in the blank space to say what will truly be done in that time period.

The difficulty is that this scheduling system is imaginary. Numerous unwritten things are competing for those blank spaces. Those are all the things we have said yes, we would do. But our own history tells us that unscheduled interruptions, emergencies, or other priorities will most likely fill those spaces. What appears to be plenty of time turns out to be no time at all.

The failure to plan and schedule our work makes us more reactive than active. It also gives us that feeling that we are behind, instead of being on top of things. The problem of imaginary scheduling causes stress, hurry-scurry days, and longer work days with more mistakes. Imaginary schedulers rely on miracle days, believing that a day of phenomenal productivity is just around the corner. Saying yes but doing no can happen because we failed to take an all-important step after we said yes: we didn't plan the work and get it into our calendar.

Reason 4. Stuff happened.

Even if we temper our optimism, start on things promptly, and do the necessary planning and scheduling, the fact is that stuff happens. Computers crash, machines break down, and things don't work as designed. People get sick, or are untruthful, or just plain stupid, and we have to wait for things that didn't get done as planned. Stuff happens.

Things do change suddenly and unexpectedly, no matter what we feel, do, or think. Competitors cut prices, clients cancel orders, and key employees get better job offers. Interruptions and emergencies happen even though we just can't afford that kind of problem right now. Murphy's Law states, "If anything can go wrong, it will." And it can go wrong even if we are doing everything right. As one manager put it, "Reality is a wake-up call."

When people say yes, they don't expect the bottom to fall out of things. Even when we make allowances for Murphy's Law, the allowances may not be enough. Sometimes stuff just happens.

Reason 5. I didn't have the right stuff.

In order to deliver what we've promised, we have to have what it takes. Some skill, ability, and talent, plus resources, information, and guidance will be required by the task we said we would do. We'll also need a determination to keep our own word despite any obstacles. All this is a matter of having the right stuff to keep our promise. If we are missing any of these key elements, there is a very high risk we'll do no, even though we said yes.

People can be very sincere and well-meaning when they say yes. But later, when it's time to do the work, they discover their feelings have changed. The desire, the commitment, or the motivation to do the work has vanished, and they probably wish they hadn't said yes. Or maybe they don't see what difference it makes, and they put it in a file and move on to something more interesting.

Still, even if you are lit up about the task and fully engaged in getting it done, you can't succeed if you don't have the wherewithal to get the job done. You need the appropriate information, resources and equipment to do what is expected. Sometimes you need permission, authority, and feedback. You need a support structure that allows you to succeed rather than one that works against you or denies access to what you need. And you need responses from other people in a timely fashion that supports the work schedule. It is difficult to move some things forward when you are waiting for others to respond.

When people say yes, they don't expect their own sincerity to disappear. They do expect they will have, or will have access to, the resources they need to do the work. But sometimes after saying yes, a person just doesn't have the right stuff for the job, and winds up doing no.

Reason 6. I didn't know (or find out) what was to be delivered.

Almost everyone pretends they know things even when they don't, and sometimes people are confused or uncertain about what it is they are supposed to deliver. It's very hard for some managers to accept that their people don't know what to do, particularly where the people have been in their job for some time. But, like it or not, some people miss deadlines because they are working in the dark. They aren't pretending, or playing dumb; sometimes they really don't know what is supposed to be delivered, when, or to whom.

How could they possibly not know? Well, for starters, people are rarely told clearly, "The deliverable should look like this." Some managers think they shouldn't have to be so specific or direct—after all, these people are professionals, or they are experienced, or they have worked here for years. These managers believe that people should "just know" what is expected of them. Some people have this same problem in their personal relationships. Have you ever heard anyone say, "I shouldn't have to tell him what I want for my birthday gift: we've been married long enough that he should know what I like by now."

The difficulty is that when you're uncertain or confused, you don't always admit it. If you're afraid you'll look bad or be embarrassed, you might not ask for the clarification and direction you need. Rather, you'll proceed based on your best guess of what you should be doing. Unfortunately, if that best guess is wrong, it won't be discovered until the delivery is made and the person expecting it is disappointed or upset. That's when you might say, "But, I thought this was what you said you wanted." By then it's too late and the damage is done.

People can also get confused when changes are made to the time line or tasks of a project. Changing requirements can result in an incomplete, or even totally wrong, product being delivered. This can happen even when everybody is sure they tracked and communicated all the vital information about changes.

Confusion and uncertainty can also arise when some people ask for things they don't really need. We know a supervisor who tells his staff, "Don't do anything for the VP until she asks you a second time. Most of the stuff she asks for isn't important enough for her to remember, and she doesn't ask for it again. Don't waste your time responding the first time around." Trying to remember cultural factors like this dilutes the instructions for the deliverable.

One last contributor to fuzzy directions is the fact that most organizations lack clear and well established methods for prioritizing deadlines. That means most people are unsure which deadlines have precedence in case of competition for scarce resources. With a large number and variety of requests and promises for deadlines, many managers and staff need a better way to determine which ones are real and which ones can wait.

Most of us think that when someone says yes to deliver something, they know what they are promising to do. But often people will say yes even when they are confused and uncertain about the exact specifications of the delivery they are promising to make. Even if they aren't sure about something, they trust they'll be able to figure things out later—and, in some cases they do. But sometimes they've said yes and done no because they didn't ask enough questions about the details.

Reason 7. I decided not to do it.

Let's not kid ourselves: sometimes people miss deadlines because they knowingly and deliberately chose to miss them. Sometimes they even knew they weren't going to do it at the very moment they said yes! They outright lied, and conned someone into believing their word was good when it wasn't. Don't expect anybody to admit it, but we all know it happens.

Why do people do that? Because they don't see any other option open to them at the time: they believe they have to say yes. Most likely, there are other things they don't know how to say, or fear the consequences if they did say them. What else might they be trying to say? Consider some options:

- I overestimated what I could get done, so I decided not to do what I promised and do another job instead. But I didn't tell you because you'd get mad.

- I couldn't get the materials I needed from someone else, so I chose to let it go. But if I'd told you about it the other person would get in trouble.

- You don't understand what I can and cannot do, and you don't let me explain it to you. It's easier just to say yes and take my lumps at the end.

This points up the biggest communication problem in most organizations today: people don't talk straight. Instead, they bury or mangle the facts. Most people like to be seen as busy, overloaded, even overwhelmed, but the fact is that very often they look at what it will take to do a job and then decide not to do it. Sometimes they will blame other people for their own inability to tell the truth: "I couldn't tell you because you'd be mad," for example.

An even uglier silent communication sometimes lies beneath the ones listed above. Imagine an instance when you deliberately did not do what you said you would do. What are you really trying to say by refusing to deliver? Some un-said communications might be:

- You should have paid more attention to me when I needed it.
- You shouldn't have embarrassed me in front of other people.
- You think you're so great and I'm nothing? Well, who's important now?

The refusal to deliver what was promised is one way of saying, "I'm here and I matter." It may be intended to let someone know they are not as important or as powerful as they seem to think. It is a communication from someone who feels powerless, and can only tip the scales of power in their favor by not doing the job. This might seem childish, and it is. But every manager must recognize that when people feel insulted, betrayed, dismissed, frustrated or powerless, they <u>do</u> become childish. Any one of us will resort to this type of behavior if all our other options seem closed.

You may never know whether someone else's doing no after saying yes is deliberate or not. But you can look for yourself and see how often you say yes when you don't mean it. Sometimes people know they lied when they said yes, and sometimes they really thought they could do it and changed their mind but didn't communicate their decision. In either case, the delivery didn't happen, and the justification might sound something like, "Other priorities came up."

Reason 8. I wouldn't ask anyone for help.

Lots of people are like the Little Red Hen: I'd rather do it myself than ask someone to help me. When people try to accomplish something on their own, they might not even notice when they need to get help. Or, if they do notice, they might not ask for the assistance, support, and resources that could make a difference in guaranteeing an on-time, high-quality result.

The most common reasons for our reluctance to recognize and ask for help are a product of ordinary human experiences. We have pride in doing things ourselves. We have been burned or betrayed by someone's help in the past and don't trust them enough to ask again this time. We don't want to be responsible for all the delegating and managing the follow-up—it's going to be too much work. Sometimes we just don't like the people we'd have to ask, and failure is preferable to working with those people.

Other common feelings will keep us from asking for help. We don't want to appear to be weak or incompetent. We're pretty sure we don't need any assistance and keep getting more focused on doing it ourselves. We don't want to share the glory if we pull it off.

Lots of people habitually play things close to the vest. They don't even tell others what they are working on, or how things are progressing. Everything is like a big secret, and without some digging you might not even know they had a deadline coming due. Sometimes people prefer to be a one-person show and won't communicate with anyone about anything they're working on if they can avoid it.

Frequently, when we say yes to a deadline we haven't thought through whether it will require the involvement of others in some way. If your tendency is to try to do tasks on your own, you are probably going to end up doing no if the task is large or complex. Even though you might insist, "I'm doing it the best way I can," failing to ask for help is sometimes working against the accomplishment of the delivery.

Reason 9. I didn't say No.

People say yes to too many things. They even say yes to things they know they should say no to, but won't. The result is they sometimes promise to do more work than they have time available in which to do it.

Since every task takes some period of time to accomplish, there is a limit to what you can put into your scheduled day. No matter how productive you are, when you say yes to everything that comes your way, something has to give. You can work longer hours (and many of you do), you can find ways to get more productive, and you can lower the quality of some of your work. But even with those techniques, at some point something will not get done as promised.

The primary culprit here is that we think of the tasks that come to us as if they were linear and independent of one another. How often do we step back to look at all the promises on our calendar, and decide which ones need to be re-negotiated or revoked? If individuals don't do this, imagine what happens with coordinating schedules and actions in a whole organization. Managers sometimes forget to coordinate priorities across different projects, or they give people additional assignments without considering what those people are already doing.

One problem with the do-everything mentality is that people ask for things without really thinking about it. People sometimes ask for things they don't need, or assign work as if people were isolated entities, instead of part of many other projects and assignments. Almost nobody looks at the larger network of assignments and communications that people are working with. As a result, it's possible that adding one simple deadline task, if the timing is right, can result in the failure to meet several other deadlines. When the overall mix of what people are working on is ignored, people and tasks get treated as if they are independent when they aren't.

At the bottom of this pile of over-committed yeses is the fact that people simply do not feel, for whatever reason, that they have the right to say no. Some are afraid of the consequences. They feel that if they tell the truth they'll pay for it. Others are just swept up in a can-do culture of high-adrenaline, high-caffeine busy-ness. It's kind of fun to keep pushing the envelope, and the excitement of being a hero can lure people beyond what their schedule or health can sustain. And of course, some bosses will not take no for an answer.

When overcommitted people say yes to the next thing, they may not know they are overcommitted. At some point they'll find out, when they can see something won't get done and they must perform some kind of triage. When we can see we are about to do no, it's time to make changes in our ability to say no too.

Reason 10. I don't think deadlines matter.

A group of mangers discussed why they weren't more successful in meeting deadlines. As they talked, they identified several of the reasons listed above, but one reason kept popping up in the conversation: "It's the culture."

When pressed to explain, they observed that in their organizations, deadlines are missed all the time. Everybody misses them. In fact, nobody is held to account for asking people to get things done by a certain time. Nobody is held to account for getting things done by their promised due date. Sometimes setting a due date for a task is so rare that nobody in the workplace even talks about whether or not they will make a deadline. Essentially, there are no deadlines—it's just not an organizational habit to use them.

If setting, tracking, and meeting deadlines is not a standard and accepted practice in an organization, then we can expect nobody is going to take a deadline very seriously. It's folly to assume people will plan their time, schedule their work, and organize to meet deadlines when no one pays attention to whether it's done or not. At some point, people realize it doesn't matter if they meet deadlines, and few people will swim against that tide.

In an organizational culture where deadlines are either regularly pushed back to accommodate events, or are missing entirely, there is no timeline management. A deadline will not be seen as real, or fixed, or important in this environment.

One manager asked us, "What's the problem? Deadlines are meant to be flexible, aren't they? It all gets done sooner or later."

When saying yes but doing no is just the way people work in the organization, no one's word means anything. It will be difficult, if not outright silly, to try to improve the on-time performance of tasks and projects in this case. Why? Because there is no dedicated process of task management to give time and promises a place of honor.

THERE ARE ALWAYS REASONS

The work that people do in organizations is never simple, even when it looks as if it is. Every task requires resources, some amount of thought, and some form of communication. Every task delivers something to someone else down, or up, the line. And every task deserves the recognition of some form of management.

When you accept a job—when you say yes to something—you agree to giving the thought, dealing with the resources, and handling the communications. You agree to deliver the goods. You say yes when you come to work. It would be pretty embarrassing to say, "Yes, I'll do it if I feel like it at the time, and if nothing else comes along, and if I'm not interrupted, and if other people do what they say, and if I'm given all the resources I need, and if I get the planning and scheduling to work out right." Maybe some of us <u>should</u> say those things, but we don't.

We just say yes. Then, after we've said yes, if we do no and don't deliver the goods, two things are certain to happen next. One: There will be consequences for the failure to deliver, and someone is going to pay, maybe a lot, maybe a little. Two: Everyone involved will have reasons to explain why the delivery didn't happen, and if the failure is serious enough you can be sure that someone will try to use more than one of the ten reasons listed above.

You can have a reputation as a reason-giver or as a Deadline Buster. Being a reason-giver is easy: anyone can always find a reason for why he or she missed a deadline. In fact, most of those reasons will be readily accepted in many organizations. So sometimes it is easier to do no, and just supply the reason. Deadline Busting requires more: you have to be willing to go beyond the reasons.

3

Going Beyond the Reasons

Sam is a consultant in a management consulting company. Every Thursday he has to produce an activity report that details the client work he did the previous week. His firm's accounting group uses the report to get their billing done correctly. Every week, Sam is late turning in his report. Every week! When asked why he keeps blowing the timeline, he says simply, "I'm so busy, I forget."

Karen is an administrative assistant at a local college. As part of her responsibilities, she is expected to attend numerous meetings. Even though she knows about each meeting well in advance, she's almost always late and often unprepared to support the agenda or discussion. When asked about it, she explains, "I know I'm late, but I frequently get calls or people stopping by my office just as I'm about to leave, and I have to deal with them. As for being prepared, I would love to be better prepared, but I'm so busy with other things I don't always have time for the last-minute things."

Alex is an investment specialist in a financial firm. He needs to complete and file his investment status summaries by the close of business every Friday so letters can be posted to clients and advisers. During the past ten weeks, Alex's report was not turned in until the following Monday or Tuesday. When asked what caused the recurring delays, Alex responds, "I didn't get the information I needed in time. I turn it over as soon as I get it."

You probably know people like Sam, Karen, or Alex. You've certainly heard those excuses when people around you miss their deadline to deliver some product, service or communication. Maybe *you've* even had occasion to use similar reasons when *you* missed a due date.

The important thing to notice is that when people miss a delivery deadline, they almost always deliver a reason instead of the result. It is such a common thing to do that many offices have learned to accept some reasons as a perfectly valid justification for a failure to deliver. Pretty soon, people begin to think that reasons are the same thing—and just as good as—delivering results.

When you or I agree to deliver something, whether it's part of our job or not, we are usually sincere about our pledge—at the moment, anyway. We mean to do what we say. But if, despite our good intentions, we don't actually get it done, we will be tempted to provide a reason in place of the results. In the face of a failure to deliver, we look for a loophole in our promise. We want a way to escape full, one-hundred per cent responsibility for the obligation we accepted when we said yes. We want a reason that will reassign the blame.

DON'T KID YOURSELF

When people fail to deliver whatever they promised, they usually defend themselves first. Reasons and justifications are what psychologists call self-serving explanations. Most of us will say what we think will make us look good to other people, so we can salvage ourselves from looking as if we've broken our word. We want to—and are usually successful, at least in our own minds—transfer blame to someone or something else. Our failure is caused by a computer glitch, a traffic jam or an unresponsive employee. Sometimes we even deny we made the promise, saying "Well, I said I'd *try* to have it done. I never said I would *definitely* have it done by then."

Giving a reason is an attempt to put ourselves in a favorable light, and to deflect or reduce the consequences for our failure. We say those things that will be readily accepted by the people around us. Most of us know what will go over well in our workplace. But our reasons cover up some other things that we do not say:

What We Say	What We Don't Say
"I wasn't able to get the client to respond on time."	"I called them at the last minute, left a phone message, and didn't call back."
"I didn't have enough time."	"I never planned out what was needed, so I didn't start to work on it until a few days ago."
"I never got the specifications from the customer."	"I knew I didn't have the specifications, but I thought the customer should have sent them to me and I didn't think I should have to ask them to do it."
"I tried to get the information, but was unsuccessful."	"I made one call, several days ago, and have done nothing since."

What We Say	What We Don't Say
"I have had nothing but interruptions this week."	"I have an open door policy and I always talk to people no matter how long they want to talk."
"Other priorities came up that I didn't expect."	"I never intended to do the work, and when something more interesting or urgent came along, I did it."

Giving a self-serving reason is a normal response when we goof up, blow the deadline, or don't do whatever we said we would do. But it's time to stop kidding ourselves. Those excuses aren't the whole truth—they're mostly just ways of pretending we aren't responsible for what happened. Our reasons help us pretend that our own decisions and behaviors were not a factor in missing the deadline.

Truthfully, we know we are pretending. In our hearts, we know there is probably some action we *might* have taken, something we could have done, that would have gotten us closer to the target. The truth is: we did not take all the necessary actions that would have delivered the results on time and gotten the job done. Or we didn't take the necessary actions at the right time, or in the right way. Or we took some other actions that got in the way of what we said we would deliver. Underneath all our reasons is a harsher truth: our own decisions and behaviors had something to do with that failed delivery.

By telling stories about all the outside factors that are to blame—events we insist are beyond our control—we might be kidding other people, at least for the moment, but not ourselves. We know we could have done something to get closer to the goal. We know we are wriggling off the hook. We hope other people will buy our story, and that they'll be polite enough to let us sell it to them. And sometimes they do. But you know what? They *will* remember that the deadline was missed. And if we think they won't, we are kidding ourselves.

Think how silly all of this really is. Sam turns his report in late every single week. Karen is consistently going to meetings late or unprepared. Alex is holding up his company's client communications. And each of them says something like, "This problem has nothing to do with me or my work habits. It's because of other people and events around me. If things were different, I'd be able to deliver on time."

What makes this silly is that, week after week, things are *not* different. Things are exactly the way they are, and they haven't changed. What Sam, Karen and Alex need to address is the way things *are*, not the way they "should" be. They have each satisfied themselves with their reasons, and have not looked deeper to discover the role played by their own decisions and behaviors. Continuing to work in the same way and produce the same errors and delays, while blaming the world around them, is a kind of insanity.[1]

CONTRIBUTORY NEGLIGENCE

There is a doctrine of law known as contributory negligence. Even if my negligence causes you an injury, you will be guilty of contributory negligence if there was some way you could have avoided the injury by taking ordinary care. In such a case, I am not entirely to blame, even though I was negligent. A court of law would apportion the blame and the damages to each of us alike.

The principle of contributory negligence can help us find ways to improve our ability to meet and beat deadlines. If you promise to do a job by Tuesday, and you don't get it done, it's possible you may be guilty of contributory negligence, no matter how good your reasons are. But, you say, "I didn't get the supplies I needed." Aha! You didn't ask for them. You didn't order them in advance. You didn't go pick them up. Your inactions are your contribution to the failure. Your lack of care is your contributory negligence.

A court of law will take it even further. If your lack of care is found to be half responsible for the failure, for instance, the court will reduce your damage award by fifty per cent. You can't blame the other guy one hundred per cent for your failure if there was something you could have done—something reasonable and demonstrating ordinary care—to prevent that failure.

This is hardball, isn't it?

Sam says he forgets. But he doesn't write things down on lists, or make notes on his calendar, or put up signs to help himself remember things. He thinks he has such a good memory he doesn't need to do that, because, as he put it, "It's a waste of time to write everything down." Sam insists that he forgets some things because he has too much to do, and he believes the solution is for him to have fewer assignments. He's kidding himself because he hasn't considered that he could adopt some new work habits and solve the problem another way. Sam also doesn't realize that other people can see what he's doing, and may decide that he's unwilling to take responsibility for performing his job responsibilities successfully. It could cost him a promotion, or worse.

---

1.   Rita Mae Brown is reported to have said "A good definition of insanity is doing the same old stuff in the same old way and expecting different results". Reported in The Reengineering Revolution: A Handbook, Michael Hammer and Steven A. Stanton, Harper Business, 1995, p. 118.

Karen holds on to her open-door policy even though that practice has made her late for almost every meeting. She doesn't see her habit of answering the phone whenever it rings, and talking to people whenever they appear at her doorway, is actually counter-productive. She doesn't know that she could answer the phone and talk to people on her own schedule, not theirs. Calls can go into voice-mail, and people can stop back later—after all, that's what happens when she is at her meetings, right? Karen's decision to take a last-minute call or visitor is a case of contributory negligence because it undermines her agreement to be on time and prepared for meetings.

Alex pulls his status summaries together when he has all the information in front of him. But he doesn't take the lead in getting that information from other people to produce an on-time result. He waits for them to give him the data sheets, saying, "When they do their job, then I can do mine. It isn't my job to remind them." But Alex's contributory negligence is that he hasn't made an effective request for what he needs, underscoring its urgency and importance, and letting people know he really-no-kidding needs it Friday morning.

Behavior patterns, with only a slight alteration, can help people keep their agreements for successful deliveries and deadlines. We can start by noticing that our own actions are contributing to the situation—and that a small change could turn it around. We all have our reasons, but we don't have to stick to them. If we do settle for reasons, our credibility pays a price, and so does our reputation at work.

Everybody knows we resist change in the workplace. But the hardest change of all is to change ourselves. How do we find out what changes we need to make? We look at our work habits—our method of operating.

WHAT IS YOUR M.O.?

When we blow a deadline, we give a reason. We hope everyone will buy it and the spotlight will move away on to something else. But our reasons, if examined more closely, can give us useful information about our M.O.

If you've ever watched a crime show on television, you've heard the term "M.O," which stands for *modus operandi*. It's Latin for "the manner of operation" and refers to the unvarying or habitual means of accomplishing something. If a murderer always leaves a tell-tale clue, that's part of his M.O. Any persistent use of certain methods and practices or any behaviors peculiar to an individual can be said to be their M.O.

- Sam's M.O. is trusting his memory and not writing things down or using his calendar to jog his memory;

- Karen's M.O. is talking to anyone who calls or comes to her office, no matter what other appointments are pending; and

- Alex's M.O. is waiting for people to give him things instead of asking for them to be delivered to meet his schedule.

One way to think about your M.O. is as your style of working, like your leadership style or your management style. It's the way you go about accomplishing things. Your M.O. includes your actions, the tools and implements you use, and all the ways you use them. If you always make lists, or you use a PDA, or you keep some of your project materials in alphabetized files and the rest in stacks on the floor, that's part of your M.O.

Everybody has a variety of formulas or recipes they've learned or acquired over time. Your M.O. helps you be successful in your work and home life. Of course, sometimes your best tricks and techniques don't work, but it can be very hard to learn new ones, so you'll tend to hang on to the ones you know. As a result, you will sometimes continue to use your M.O. even when it doesn't work.

Your M.O. is a set of work habits, automatic patterns of actions that are reinforced by repeated use. You may not even know you're using them; they just seem to happen. And that's the point. Your M.O. can be applied unthinkingly in all kinds of circumstances, sometimes when it isn't appropriate or effective. Even the way you read this sentence, the way you view this book, and the time and place you read it, are all a part of your M.O.

Apart from behaviors, another crucially important aspect of your M.O. is the props you use—the different tools you use to get things done. Look around yourself right now and see if you can spot some of them: your particular kind of pens, pencils, coffee cup, note paper, desk, chair, computer, software, fax machine, phone, schedule, plans, meeting agendas, etc. Depending on your M.O., you'll prefer some tools over other ones: you might like to use paper calendars and email instead of electronic calendars and live messaging, for instance.

The third and final aspect of your M.O. is that is relates to your reasons for missing deadlines. If you say, "I forgot," your M.O. probably doesn't support remembering things very well. If you say, "I have to...," your M.O. probably doesn't include the ability to say no to people or to make other arrangements for certain things. If you say, "They didn't...," then your M.O probably doesn't have much muscle in the area of asking other people to do things. Your reasons for not delivering on-time results can tell you something about your unconscious habits and practices.

Your M.O. is the chief hero—or culprit—of whatever reputation you have for effectiveness, timeliness, and performance in your workplace. A little examination of your work habits, props, and explanations for failures will help you be more responsible for your successes and failures. That responsibility is a vital component in Deadline Busting. Discovering your M.O. is a good place to start toward improving your own performance.

YOU CAN CHANGE YOUR M.O.

Where your M.O. fits your work conditions and job requirements, you are successful. Where it doesn't, you have problems and possibly even failure. The good news is that by looking at your problems and failures, you'll be able to learn something about your M.O. Here's what Jonathan said about his M.O.

> My M.O. consists of me doing everything I can, hands-on, to meet a deadline. Once I finish my part of it and pass it off to the next guy, or rely on someone else to get something done, I consider the item out of my hands. At that point, if it doesn't get done completely or the right way or on time, I can clearly point the finger at someone else. I say, "There was nothing I could have done," or, "It was out of my hands by then." This is the way I limit my responsibility, and protect myself from being blamed for the bigger job or the more complicated communications.

This is a useful observation. When Jonathan noticed the M.O. he used to protect himself from being blamed, he was able to see that maybe he was limiting himself in other ways too. Here's more from Jonathan:

> I just realized that when I look at only the 'little picture' of what I am directly responsible for, I am causing a problem for my boss. He wasn't able to keep to his plans and timelines because certain pieces were dropped out. I see that when I take my piece, then just do it and hand it off, I'm not looking at how to have the whole deadline met. I'm just looking at my own little deadline, but I see I could go above and beyond that piece. I could look at a bigger picture, because all those other pieces that are related to my piece are what add up to the whole thing. They all need to be done on time, not just mine. I think I could have a bigger impact than I've been having.

If you want to shoot for the moon and be someone who consistently meets or beats deadlines, you'll have to upgrade your M.O. It requires telling the truth about what you do, and don't do, and looking to see how your own behavior contributes to the results you are getting with the habits you've got. Changing your M.O. requires that you go beyond reasons, confront your own contributory negligence, and see a bigger picture.

...*But, You Gotta Want To*

Your habits have been around long enough to make themselves at home in your life and your world. As a result, you'll need a compelling reason to change any of them. Start looking: what's in it for you? Why should you change anything about the way you work? What would be the objective for making a change? Here are some sample objectives to get you started:

- Get a better performance review

- Get a good recommendation from a supervisor

- Be recognized or receive a performance award

- Have data to support a promotion

- Personal pride and satisfaction

- Build justification for advancement up the ladder or into something new

Changing your M.O. will be much smoother if you have a direct and understandable benefit for doing it. It's far easier to continue doing what you've always done: giving reasons and hoping things will turn out well. But if you can find some likely rewards for making the change, you can give yourself the energy of purpose. Jonathan again:

> It finally clicked for me that if my boss does better, he'll see me as more of an asset than he does right now. If he saw I could coordinate or help orchestrate more things, it could also help me get a lot more interesting work. I'd like to be more of a big-picture guy instead of an analyst. The bigger variety of the work I could do at a higher level job is as attractive to me as the bigger paycheck is.

When you realize that you M.O. is behind you own success or failure, it's a wake-up call. Suddenly you can see a pathway to making some changes, even though you might not know exactly how to go about it. Those insights can add up to a whole new relationship with your work and your workplace activities, as Jonathan discovered.

> I realized this for the first time last night. I've had a "non-convincing attitude" about my work. I've been willing to promise only what I could do personally, hands-on. I couldn't convince myself or anyone else that I'd be responsible for getting things done unless they were on my desk or in my portfolio. That needs to change. I need to do more about meeting the 'big picture' deadline even after my part is done. I need to be more convincing that things will get done and then do all I can to have them happen. In the end, the chips will fall where they may, but I need to eat, drink, and sleep success. Not success for my piece, but success in meeting the deadline.

...And It Takes Practice

Habits don't change just because we have an insight about them. If it were that easy, we could all just read a book and re-vamp ourselves. New habits are acquired through practice, and practice requires more than understanding. Practice takes patience and persistence. Bobby Knight, the college basketball coach, is reported to have said, "The key is not the will to win...everybody has that. It's the will to *prepare* to win that is important." Preparing to win means practice.

No one goes directly from concept to mastery in one step. Things may even get worse before they get better. Whenever you try something new it disrupts other things, and that can be disconcerting to you and to other people. Everyone around you is used to you and your ways, and when you start new practices, it can be an annoyance. That's why you need to put your goal in front of yourself: a raise, a promotion or a performance evaluation. You'll be rocking the boat, so be sure you get something for your trouble.

DEADLINE BUSTING—IT'S YOUR CHOICE

There are two ways people relate to their working life. The first way is to see work as being mostly a response to other people and circumstances. People who are passive about their work may (or may not) do their best with whatever comes their way, and then wait till the next demand comes along. In a sense, their responsibility starts at their in-box and goes only as far as their out-box. Many people won't go looking for more work beyond either of those boundaries. If a deadline isn't met, or a delivery isn't right, then the reason lies elsewhere. And, if the company, or the boss, sets a goal to improve on-time delivery, then they are responsible to change the way things work.

The second way is to see your work as if it's up to you to make things happen. You can operate as if the company's goals and the boss' goals are your goals too. There is no particular reason to choose this way. It can help you advance yourself, such as by getting a promotion or having more stimulation from learning new things at work. But some people choose an active relationship to work just because they want to play: they like to find new ways to succeed, and to win the game of on-time deliveries.

This active path is for those of us who take pride in what we do, who want our word to mean something, and who are willing to discover and confront what it takes to consistently meet a deadline. We try to make the goals, and when something doesn't work, we try something else—and we keep trying new things until we make the target. We'd rather take charge of our work and make things happen than wait and hope for things to turn out.

As Jonathan says, "In the end, the chips will fall where they may." There are no guarantees, even when you play full out, that you'll always beat the deadline. Even the most reliable delivery services like FedEx and UPS will miss an occasional delivery promise.

But once you know that it's your own choice whether to make the delivery or make up a reason, why not live a little and play for the win? You have the power to upgrade your Modus Operandi, and that's the key to deadline busting. Now it's only a matter of deciding to play.

4

The Tips

Okay, you've decided to take on the task of upgrading your M.O., and to develop yourself in deadline busting. But where do you start? The people who worked with us in creating Deadline Busting found the best idea is to start with what you know *isn't* working around you in your job or your work environment. First, those are the places you might have the most motivation to make a change. And second, that's where you'll get the most reward for making a change.

How to start? Imagine that the collection of tips on the following pages is a tray of appetizers. Start by trying the ones that seem most intriguing or attractive to you. Skip the ones that look distasteful or unwise for your particular situation at this time. You can always come back later; they might look very attractive in another time and place. You know yourself and your workplace better than anyone else, so you are most likely to know what will work for you and what won't. Select an appetizer, or two, or ten. Test them in your workplace, with your co-workers, and see what happens.

TIP 1: HAVE A SPECIFIC DUE DATE AND TIME

Be sure you have a specific date and time
by when the product, project, or action is due.

If you don't have these,
then you don't have a deadline—
you have a "whenever."

This tip sounds obvious, doesn't it? But try this experiment: Make a list of every assignment or project you have where someone else is expecting something from you. Then review the list to answer this question: "How many of these have a clear and specific due date and time?

Set a specific date for each assignment to be due. A specific due date is "January 23, 2025." A vague due date is, "the end of January," or "as soon as possible" or "next week if you can."

Unclear due dates and times lead to misunderstandings. The meaning of "as soon as possible" will vary with circumstances and interruptions and personal moods or urgencies.

If you don't have a specific deadline, you have a "whenever." A "whenever" gets done whenever they bug you enough for it, whenever you find time to work on it, whenever you feel guilty enough to do it, etc. "Whenevers" are stressful, because they give you ever-looming due dates to carry around. Lighten your load and pick a date.

It tightens things even more when you have a specific time. A clear and unambiguous deadline would look like this: "The wireless program is to be handed over by 3:30 P.M. January 23, 2025." Sounds pretty attention-getting, doesn't it?

And that's the point: to have a due date and time that gets attention. The rigor of a timeline like that encourages you—and other people—to organize and schedule the necessary work to get a high-quality, on-time delivery. If the due date is vague, you're more likely to accept being vague about the steps to take, the sequence of tasks involved, and getting it all scheduled in a workable way. Start right: have a specific due date and time.

TIP 2: MAKE COUNTEROFFERS WHEN NECESSARY

When given a deadline you know you <u>cannot</u> meet,
propose an alternative you can meet.
That's called making a counteroffer.

If you don't counteroffer when you know something cannot be done,
you're setting up many people for a failure.

What do you do when someone asks you to do something you know you cannot get done? Do you say yes and hope things will work out somehow? Do you say yes, planning to deal with the consequences later? Or do you say yes and break other promises you've made for on-time performance?

A better way to deal with the situation is to make a counteroffer. That's where you say, "I can't do A, but I can do B". For example, say, "I can't get it for you by 5:00 P.M. today, but I can get it for you by 3:00 P.M. tomorrow." Another type of counteroffer is, "I can't do A unless B happens." For example, say, "I won't be able to do that today unless we can extend the due date on Project B by at least a day."

A counteroffer communicates three important things. First, it says that you are not currently in a position to accept their request as it is given to you. Second, it says that you are willing to work something out. Third, it says that you will be responsible for what you promise, because it prevents the need for excuses later on.

A counteroffer isn't just saying, "I'm too busy," or, "I don't have time." To be effective, counteroffers must be made with integrity because you are negotiating an alternative promise. You are offering to do something, and you may also be re-negotiating the due dates of one or more other projects.

Counteroffers can be very effective. You may not get all the leeway you ask for, but that should remind you to ask for as much as you think you need. It's worth giving counteroffers a try, even if you think the people around you are pretty inflexible. You just might be surprised.

TIP 3: CONVERT EXPECTATIONS INTO AGREEMENTS

Don't risk being held to account for things you didn't know about.

Take the time to find out what people expect you to do, and what they expect you to deliver. Then make all of that a part of your planning to meet and beat the deadline.

Look at each of your current assignments. Are you confident you are a hundred per cent clear about what is expected of you in every case? Is everyone else involved in the project also clear about what you expect of them? Or are you assuming things, like that you'll be able to figure it out later, or they already know all about it?

Assumptions and expectations are silent standards. You take a big risk when you assume other people know what to do. If creativity is desirable, it's fine to give a general direction. But if there are specific requirements that matter, get them spelled out.

Take the time to get specific. What should the delivered product or communication look like? What are the components? When do they need to be ready? Who must be involved? Don't take a chance: assume nothing is obvious.

Remember: everyone associated with your deadline has their own expectations and assumptions. Some people expect you to ask for their advice, others want to be kept informed, and some want only to be involved in an emergency. Warning: people expect you to operate according to their expectations even if you don't know what they are! Ask people to take time with you to spell out their expectations.

Turning expectations into agreements gives you the opportunity to say whether you can or cannot do what they ask. If something new comes up later, you can always say, "I didn't agree to that, but I'm willing to consider it." You want to avoid having to say, "I didn't know you needed that," or, "I thought this is what you wanted".

Reduce your risk by taking time to turn unspoken expectations into clear agreements that everyone can see and understand.

TIP 4: RECONCILE THE NEEDS OF MULTIPLE CUSTOMERS

If you have more than one type of customer, be sure you find out from each of them what they want the end result to be. Help them get what they need to achieve their goals or objectives.

Who is the "customer" for the deadline you were given? Is it the boss who assigned you the deadline? Is it someone else who will use whatever product or service you are going to produce? Or is it a third party who is paying for the end product but will not be the user? Believe it or not, it might be all three!

If you have only one customer, and it's your boss, your job is easy: just get the specifics and you're good to go. But if there are multiple customers with various expectations, you'll need to do all the homework to clarify their needs up front. This includes specifying the meaning of technical words and phrases, agreeing on policies and common procedures, and confirming all the details of performance and delivery.

Assuming the expectations of one customer group will translate to another can also be very costly. If your boss asks you to "draft up the specs" for a job, for example, you probably want to find out who is going to use them, and for what, and how they will know if the final specs are terrific. If possible, provide your customers with a mock-up of the final product to further uncover any unspoken, but presumed obvious requirements.

Deadline busters will operate from the standpoint that their job is to make the customer look good. When you work with every player who is authorizing, using and/or paying for the result, you can set up the project for a win that serves the customers' objectives.

The more you learn about why the deliverable is important to your boss, the user(s), and the payer(s), the more likely you are to see the biggest picture. That perspective helps you better serve all your customers, which is the ultimate win for everyone.

TIP 5: DISCOVER AND SATISFY ALL KNOWN RESOURCE CONSTRAINTS

To bust a deadline you need to know all the resources—and all the constraints on those resources—that relate to the job.

If you fail to satisfy constraints, then you are too expensive.

Few of us are given a blank check for meeting a deadline. And since most deadlines require resources—personnel, equipment and materials, and budget—those things must be managed too. It's important to learn all the constraints and limitations that apply.

The availability and use of resources will affect your plans on how to go about meeting the deadline. It's one thing to meet a deadline where you have been authorized to do whatever it takes, with a bottomless budget to match. But most often you have to extend existing resources and sometimes those are already spread thin. Knowing your limitations up front, or adjusting plans as soon as they become known, can save you time on the back end. It's better to know what you can and can't use than to build plans on hope or ignorance.

<u>Personnel.</u> Who is available for working on this deadline? Is overtime allowed? Can consultants be used? Can temporary hires be used? Can you take people from other projects? Are some people fully yours or only partially yours?

<u>Equipment & Material.</u> Can new equipment be purchased? Will equipment and materials be shared with other projects, or are they dedicated? Must purchases be made through existing procedures using current vendors or is there a special process?

<u>Budget.</u> Are additional funds available? If so, what are the limitations on their use? Whose budget will be charged for each type of cost? What happens if existing budgets are exhausted?

The sooner you know your resource constraints, the better you can plan and organize accordingly. You will have fewer surprises and setbacks, and a better chance of success.

Tip 6: Know the Deadlines of Your Deadline-Giver

Deadlines are rarely given in isolation. They are almost always part of another project or a larger strategic objective.

When you understand what's at stake in the bigger picture, you can make decisions with a smarter, wider perspective.

So, someone just gave you a deadline. Do you know what deadline he or she is trying to meet? What is the deadline-giver's tightest time and delivery constraint? You might want to learn that. Why? There are three reasons.

First, it allows you to see how your deadline fits into a bigger picture. Your success or failure will affect other things, and you need to know what they are. You want to be able to plan for any ripple effects that could have far-reaching consequences.

Second, it's always useful to know what other people are up against. It gives you a better appreciation for what you have been asked to do and why it is of value. It also lets you take small actions to give the other person a boost in case you're feeling generous.

Third, it helps prevent those situations where you push people to meet a deadline and then find out the deadline wasn't real. You can't plan your work accurately if you unknowingly build in someone else's padding or exaggerated sense of urgency.

It's demoralizing to invest in meeting a schedule only to learn it was a bogus deadline. Even if you blame the deadline-giver for misleading you, you'll lose credibility and trust with the people you pushed. They'll assume you knew, or believe you should have known, and their suspicion will make it harder for you to rally them next time around.

Know what you're working with; whenever possible, learn the deadlines of your deadline-giver so you can plan the work in a way that uses all resources appropriately.

TIP 7: HONOR PEOPLE'S FEELINGS, BUT DON'T YIELD THE GAME TO THEM

It's appropriate for people to have feelings about a job.
But be sure people know their feelings will take a back seat
to meeting the deadline.

Feelings, thoughts and moods are fine,
but meeting the deadline is the greater game.

When we see a yield sign on the highway, it means one driver surrenders the right of way to another stream of traffic. Any driver who fails to yield will risk causing an accident. Similarly, at times each of us must yield our preferences, likes or dislikes, and moods to accomplish something we've agreed to do.

Individual quirks, preferences, and ego-needs will always be a kind of noisy static buzzing around the work of producing an on-time result. But those working on the deadline should understand one thing: if their ego comes into conflict with the velocity of the assignment, they'll need to give it up and yield to the deadline.

This is particularly true for the person managing to achieve the deadline. We tend to think, "If I'm the one in charge, things should go my way." The truth is the opposite: a good leader is a master at surrendering personal interests to a greater game. You may have to give up your attitudes or gripes even more often than your staff will.

Make sure people working with you understand that you respect their personal feelings and preferences, but that you won't allow those to interfere with meeting the deadline. If bad moods hold up progress, they need to be set aside to focus on keeping the promise. This doesn't mean you ignore personal needs or well-being issues. It does mean petty grievances will not be honored at the same level as professional agreements.

It's best to have visible measures that allow everyone to see progress being made toward reaching the deadline. Visible objectivity can help trump intangible moods.

Tip 8: Be Willing to Give Up Your Way

There are many ways to meet most deadlines. Some you know and some you don't. Let other people contribute their good ideas.

Allowing other people to invent their own ways to meet the deadline adds new energy to the whole project.

When you work on something, does it have to be done one particular way? Or are you free to go along with other people's suggestions? Can you give up doing things your way, or do you insist that people do things the way you think is best?

It's helpful to remember that there are many ways to accomplish an outcome. Even though some ways are not as efficient as others, there's rarely one and only one way to do anything. That's why it's important to keep your focus on what you are trying to accomplish as you allow more flexibility and experimentation in the ways it gets done. This is particularly true when the deadline involves something you haven't done before.

If everyone understands the deadline's objectives and constraints, it will be to your advantage to let them generate new methods. At times your experience will count, but don't let it dominate their work or it will suffocate creativity and cleverness. Make suggestions when asked, but don't stifle people's energy.

If people begin to believe that working with you gives them a chance to unfold their wings, they'll expand their participation and contribution. This is a great way to develop people and get things done at the same time. And if problems arise or you ever need them to perform above and beyond the normal, you're more likely to get their full support.

The point is to accomplish the deadline while satisfying all the constraints and limitations that apply. You can be firm about producing the end results, while being willing to loosen your attachment to some of the processes. This might tap potential talent you didn't know you had.

TIP 9: BOX YOURSELF IN BY "BURNING THE BOATS"

If people don't believe they have to meet the deadline, they won't do everything they can to meet it.

Let people know the deadline is real and that you won't entertain alternatives to meeting it.

When Caesar invaded England, he burned his boats to let his men know that there was no way home. The only options were victory or death. For most of us, the idea of cutting off all retreat is unnerving. We like to keep our options open, to have a back door escape as a way out.

This escape hatch can undermine success. When it comes to deadlines, you want to cultivate a no-alternative attitude. Root out any talk about "we'll try", or "we'll do our best", or "we'll see". These wishy-washy, uncommitted conversations are not idle chatter; they undermine meeting the deadline.

Loopholes and vagueness lead people to believe that all they have to do is work hard. This leads to the erroneous conclusion that cost overruns and time extensions, or some other variety of failure, will be acceptable. Once this thinking takes hold, it quickly becomes a cultural norm that is difficult to turn around. One manager, when asked why he regularly missed his deadlines, said, "Well, deadlines are flexible aren't they?"

If you're serious about meeting a deadline, take a tip from Caesar: he wasn't interested in trying, he was interested in conquest. As Yoda, the Jedi master in Star Wars, said to Luke Skywalker "Do or do not. There is no try."

You want more than half-hearted efforts from people. Find a way to burn the boats and focus attention on busting the deadline. Take every opportunity to set the tone: success is the goal and failure is not an option.

TIP 10: OWN THE DEADLINE

Don't be a victim to a deadline.
Own it as your own and put yourself in charge.

Owning your deadline increases the chance of success
and reduces resentment all around.

Look at the deadlines you have and ask yourself, "Whose deadlines are these?" Are they unequivocally your own commitments, or are they demands foisted off on you by someone else? When your relationship to a deadline is proprietary, you are determined to win for your own success. This gives a different quality to your communications, your planning, and your resource management than if you're operating as a victim to someone else's demands.

Have you ever noticed how protective and concerned you are about "your stuff", all the things you own? Most of us take better care of the things we own than the things we rent or lease, just because they are ours. The same is true with a deadline.

One good test: if it's okay with you if the deadline isn't met with a high quality on-time delivery, then it's not really yours.

One supervisor told us, "I make *all* deadlines mine, not something I am doing for someone else. If I think it's theirs, it seems heavier somehow." When you don't own the deadline, it will own you. You'll resent the imposition, or look for shortcuts that could compromise the quality or delivery.

When you own the deadline, you are responsible for it, and people know it. You won't be interested in making excuses. When you get yourself engaged at the level of ownership, you put yourself in charge. It's your game now, not something you're putting up with, and you'll be able to take the reins to organize for meeting the deadline.

TIP 11: GIVE IT YOUR FULL ATTENTION

People can tell how important a deadline is by how much attention you give to it. When you're working on a deadline, work on it, don't multi-task.

Let people know you're on top of the issues and engaged in the deadline's accomplishment.

"I never could have done what I have done without the habits of punctuality, order and diligence, without the determination to concentrate myself on one subject at a time."

—Charles Dickens

If you want to know what's important to someone, watch where they spend their time and their money. It's certainly true in organizations. People notice what managers talk about, measure, and reward. That's how people know what the score is, how to decide what's most important to work on, and how to know what they can ignore.

If your deadline is important to you, give it all your attention. Talk about it at meetings, schedule time to focus on it, and work to obtain resources for it. People will notice if you're like a dog with a bone instead of someone with only a passing interest in the success of the delivery.

Giving one deadline your full attention doesn't mean you ignore all other deadlines. It means when you're working on one thing don't try to do everything else at the same time. Give yourself permission to let voicemail handle your calls. Turn off your email. Close your door.

We know one product manager who puts a sign on his door saying, "If you're not here about the new launch, don't even THINK about knocking." His focus helps to get other people focused too, and demonstrates that the deadline is real and important, and that he's working to stay on top of it.

If you have multiple deadlines, give each one your full attention when you are working on it. If you don't, other people won't either. While "parallel processing" is popular, concentration wins the day for busting deadlines. It also helps you have fewer mistakes and more milestone successes.

TIP 12: BE CONVINCED AND CONVINCING ABOUT YOUR SUCCESS

Act as if you can't fail. Talk as if the outcome is certain and worthwhile.

If there is any doubt, people will find it. If they find it, they'll use it as an excuse for letting up. Don't give failure an opening.

Do you believe you can successfully meet each one of your deadlines? Not that you're unrealistic, but are you sure if everyone does what needs to be done, things will go well? Or are you wondering whether or not you can succeed?

If you don't believe you'll make the deadline, other people will wonder too. And if they aren't sure they can succeed, they may hesitate to invest themselves fully. People may be reluctant to take chances, either with their time or their abilities, if they aren't sure this project is going to be both worthwhile and a winner.

This doesn't mean being a Pollyanna, or making up tall tales. But it doesn't hurt to do two things. First, if you aren't sure it's going to succeed, investigate your concerns. There may be some legitimate areas you need to clarify: timelines, resources, customers, etc. Make sure you get yourself convinced you've got a plan for winning.

Second, accept the fact that part of the job is being a cheerleader for the deadline. Don't let the atmosphere around the deadline get polluted with negative talk or sloppy meetings and materials.

Being convinced and convincing about success doesn't mean you know what will happen. But watch your attitude and the way you present the job to others. Don't give people your worries—it doesn't help them do their job. Give people the sense that the work can be done and it's worth doing well. Put a good spin on things that happen, even if they seem threatening. Don't let yourself or others give up, even when things look bad.

Tip 13: Take Care of Your People

Anyone you depend on to meet a deadline is one of "your people".
If you want their best work, learn how things are going for them.

If people think you don't care about them,
they lose respect for your objectives.

A common mistake when working on a deadline is failing to take an interest in the work situation of the people helping you produce the results. When you are on deadline you may become so task-oriented that you become too serious, aloof, or unapproachable. If you don't notice what's happening with the people on the job, you risk losing both productivity and good will in your workplace.

Don't blindly demand, but check with people before giving an assignment. Learn what they're working on, and help them make necessary adjustments to their work plans. It does you no good if they say yes, but do no.

People have other commitments in life outside their job. They get stressed by a variety of things, and can have all manner of troubles doing their work. Sometimes you may think your deadline is all that matters, or that no one is as busy or working as hard as you are. It's important to remember other people have other demands, different work habits, and challenges that we can't see.

You may need to protect some people from the requests of others. Go to bat for them. Make counteroffers where necessary. If you concentrate exclusively on accomplishing the deadline and don't attend to what other people are dealing with, you run the risk that their energy will wilt or disperse. If people feel they are being taken for granted, or that you don't care, they can become more focused on their own complaints than on your objectives—and you'll pay for it.

If your deadline is going to impose a hardship, let people know that. Remember to say thank you, even when you think you shouldn't have to do it. A little genuine concern and attention will go a long way.

TIP 14: KNOW YOUR SILVER BULLETS

If you want to kill a werewolf, you use a silver bullet. If you want to stop productivity, there are silver bullets that will do that too.

**To avoid being stopped, know your silver bullets,
and make friends with them.**

Folklore has it that if you want to kill a werewolf, you do it with a silver bullet. The story is that a mere threat of being shot with a silver bullet will stop one in its tracks. Ordinary people are also stopped in their tracks, sometimes with a single word or phrase, or tone of voice. Those are silver bullets that stop productivity in its tracks.

A silver bullet is unique to each person; it's whatever way you don't want people to think of you or talk about you. If you're afraid people will think you're arrogant or inconsiderate, then any hint they're thinking it will stop you cold. If you're proud of your honesty and integrity, or your intelligence and open-mindedness, or your principles and values, then you can be brought down by someone suggesting you're dishonest, stupid, biased, or unprincipled.

Silver bullets are very effective; they always alter our behavior. We know a manager who won't ask his boss for anything because he doesn't want to seem weak. Another friend doesn't want to be thought of as pushy, so she avoids delegating any assignments and does everything herself. The threat of a silver bullet stops our work and focuses our attention on dealing with the insult.

The solution? Get to know your silver bullets. Think of the worst thing someone could say about you behind your back. What is the most precious aspect of your reputation? What is the worst trait to have in your workplace? The answers may show you potential silver bullets that others can use to control you, or steer you toward making reactive decisions. Their control can jeopardize your deadline.

Consider disarming the bullets. Maybe those accusations don't deserve the power you have given them, or the power you have given away to other people's opinions.

TIP 15: MAKE FREQUENT AND BOLD REQUESTS AND PROMISES

The velocity of any project is a function of the number and magnitude of requests and promises made.

To increase the rate of progress on any deadline, ask for more, and more often.

The velocity of progress toward any deadline is a direct result of two things: (1) the frequency of requests and promises made, and (2) the magnitude of what is asked for and what is promised. Research shows that the more frequent and bigger the requests and promises, the faster things happen.

Requests and promises (which include threats) are the only form of speech specifically intended to produce action and results. A request asks another person to do something or to make something happen by a particular time. For example, "Please call Zano's and order a pizza for the 1:00 P.M. staff meeting today." A promise tells another person that you will do something or make something happen by a particular time. For example, "I will call the customer and confirm specifications for the ABX process by 3:00 P.M. today".

When you increase the frequency of making requests and promises, say from one a day to two a day, it also increases the number of opportunities for actions or results. When you increase the amount of action or the size of the results you ask for, you also increase the velocity of whatever you're working on. A request that staff make ten phone calls in the next hour, rather than the normal five, will stir up more action and more potential results. Making promises will also stir *you* into action. Increasing *both* the frequency and magnitude of what you ask for *and* promise produces an even greater effect on velocity, progress, and outcomes.

We're sometimes afraid to ask for more, but children who want ice cream know the secret: they don't give up. Kids are little masters of making frequent and bold requests, and they'll make big promises to get what they want. Take the tip: make more requests, more often, to more people, for more actions and more results in a shorter time.

Be prepared to have people say you're unreasonable, pushy, or demanding—potential silver bullets. But to add velocity to your situation, defang that bullet. Go ahead and ask for whatever ice cream you think will get things going.

TIP 16: BE ZEALOUS ABOUT KEEPING
AGREEMENTS

Meeting deadlines depends on people keeping their agreements and doing what they said they would do.

Encourage people to respect the idea that keeping agreements matters.

Keeping agreements is the foundation for meeting deadlines. Every time we say yes to a deadline, or make a promise or accept a request, we have created an agreement with someone. It might be as simple as agreeing to make reservations for a lunch meeting or as complex as developing a production plan or installing a computer system. But in any case, you're on the hook for doing something the minute you nod your head or mutter, "Yeah, okay."

Those agreements matter. People count on us to do what we said, and if we don't do it they'll have a judgment about our reliability that won't serve us well in the future. Similarly, we depend on others to do what they say they'll do. If you've ever had to follow up on an undelivered shipment, an unanswered question, or an unpaid invoice, you know agreements are important to the fabric of life.

We don't trust people who don't keep their agreements. And we lose credibility when we don't keep ours. Even if people have a good explanation for what happened, we're probably still left with some consequences left over from their dropping the ball.

When you are working to a deadline, every missed agreement is a potential for disaster. To make a timeline, you can't afford to have people take their promises casually. A climate of accountability is essential for meeting deadlines, and that depends on having a positive regard for keeping agreements.

When agreements are broken, be zealous about getting to the bottom of what happened so you can learn what will help avoid similar situations in the future. Good cleanup is another way to honor your promises and strengthen your credibility.

Tip 17: When Things Go Wrong, Review and Recommit

It's easy to lose interest or give up when things go wrong.
Better to recommit to the game and take a fresh look
at where things went off course.

Those times when mistakes pile up are precisely when you
need to increase your engagement.
Renew your promise and recommit to the delivery.

When things are going well, it's fairly easy to stay engaged, focused, and on the job. It's easier to talk about success than it is to talk about failures. It's also easier to get more people involved and keep things moving when you're winning. As the cliché goes, "Nothing succeeds like success."

But, you can lose your focus and momentum when things start getting tough or when you have a setback. It can be discouraging to work on things that are not going well. You are more likely to be upset or frustrated, and less likely to find ways to talk about problems without sounding negative about the whole thing. Sometimes it's tempting to sweep things under the rug.

The longer you put off taking a fresh look at the problems, the harder it is to bring yourself to work on them. When things are going wrong, results are unfavorable, or mistakes are piling up, it's time to stop and look newly at what you have committed to.

The biggest risk is losing sight of what you're trying to achieve. Take the time to review your promise, the deadline, and the delivery. Remind yourself of what you set out to accomplish. This is the time to make note of everything you think might help get things back on track. Do you need changes in resources? Communications? Timing? Get specific about your course-correction ideas and the actions you need to take.

It is important to recover your commitment to your promise. Re-commit to the delivery. Tell the truth about where you are, without wishful thinking, then decide on your actions for recovery, rally the troops, and get into action.

Tip 18: Don't Give Excuses When Things Go Wrong

Don't blame other people or outside circumstances when things don't go as expected.

Blaming undermines your credibility.
It also reduces people's willingness to support you.

What do you do when you cannot deliver what you said you would? It's human nature to want to find someone or something else to blame. We want to look good and avoid looking bad, particularly to people who are important to us.

We often want to avoid responsibility when things don't work right, or when something breaks, gets lost or is forgotten. And almost everyone will buy our story. After all, everyone agrees there are things going on beyond our control. It's easy to blame suppliers, the computer system or the union.

Shifting the blame for problems is what psychologists call self-serving attributions—attributing blame elsewhere to save ourselves. The problem with self-serving attributions is that they are so transparent. Everyone can tell when you're trying to dodge blame. Blame-shifting is something we learned—and learned to recognize—when we were children. So when we do it we look childish. Even if people are polite and accept the excuse, they know they're talking to a nervous child. Besides, the people you are blaming might catch wind of it, and they'll resent the accusation.

Here's an idea: when things go wrong, step up to the plate. Tell people what *you* could have said or done to prevent or reduce the problem. This is a big and dangerous idea—very radical, but also very impressive.

A deadline buster works to avoid excuse-making and blame-placing. Look to see what you might have done to prevent things from going wrong, and learn what you could do differently in the future. It's a tough stance to take, but it's very grown up, and it builds trust and increases effectiveness.

TIP 19: ADMIT YOUR MISTAKES

Everyone makes mistakes, but not everyone admits it.

Admitting your mistakes helps other people see a safe environment for learning and making improvements.

Many of us have difficulty remembering, let alone admitting mistakes. In part it's because whatever we did we thought was the right thing to do at the time. We didn't set out to make a mistake. So, we remember our good intentions, which makes it hard to see our actions from the perspective that we made a mistake.

You know you are not always right. You misunderstand, miscalculate, and misinterpret things all the time. But making a mistake is embarrassing. You and everybody else hates to admit a mistake and risk looking stupid or foolish, and perhaps undermine your authority or cause people to question your competence.

Admitting a mistake takes courage. In fact, it's easier to place blame than admit a mistake. So when you do admit a mistake, it stands out as something unusual, even special. You have to respect someone who can step up and say, "My fault, I misjudged that one."

Most people forgive a mistake, especially if the person who did it owns up and shoulders the blame. Ownership ends the discussion and focuses people on solving whatever is next. But when a mistake is made and no one will own it, people keep thinking about it, wondering what caused it and why no one will admit it. It sucks people's energy away just trying to understand a universe where mistakes happen out of thin air.

Encourage people to own their mistakes, and be a model for doing that yourself. Deadlines are at risk every time a mistake is made and not reported and owned. The pain of admitting a mistake is not as bad as the pain of a missed deadline.

TIP 20: IDENTIFY AND PUBLICIZE YOUR FINAL AUTHORITIES

Rather than have people chase all over to get answers to questions, let them know from whom you will accept answers.

Establish the final authorities for different aspects of your deadline, then stand by the answers they provide.

To whom should people go when they have technical questions? Who should answer their questions about finances, contracts, software programming, labor law, personnel policies, product pricing or anything else that could arise while working on the deadline? Who are your final authorities?

At times people will have questions in specialized areas outside their expertise or yours. Is it okay for them to go anyone for their answers, or do you want them to get their answers from particular people in whom you have confidence?

In a deadline pinch, people will get answers to technical questions from wherever they can, including people without the appropriate background, position or credentials. Rather than search out the experts, people often go to someone they know or someone who is nearby.

Sometimes getting an answer is not good enough. You want the best possible answer from someone whose reputation you trust, someone you establish as your final authority. For technical or specialty areas related to the deadline, identify all the people you'll accept as the final authority. They have the knowledge and information, the expertise or authority you want.

Once you've identified your final authorities, make sure you've gotten their permission to use them as a resource for questions. Then tell everyone who they are so they know who to go to for answers. Then don't accept final answers in those areas from anyone else, and of course, don't appeal the answers they give you to anyone else.

TIP 21: ACCOUNT FOR INTERRUPTIONS IN YOUR SCHEDULE

Interruptions are a predictable part of today's work world and need to be accounted for when you're planning to complete something.

Failing to account for interruptions costs you more than missing a deadline. It also dramatically increases your stress.

How much time do you spend every day dealing with interruptions? Studies show that people at work are interrupted an average of every eight minutes—about sixty times a day. If every interruption took only two minutes of time (and many take much more than that), then about two hours of every day is used in dealing with interruptions.

Those statistics won't match your world exactly, but the point is that interruptions are predictable. People treat them as surprises, or as nuisances they cannot control. But if you know that interruptions will cost you one to two hours a day, you can account for this time as you plan to meet your deadline.

Project managers know there will be interruptions, so they build slack into the project schedule to account for unexpected events. But most individuals don't do that with their personal schedules. Although you know interruptions will occur, you may not remember that when scheduling your tasks.

Research shows that people tend to make optimistic estimates of time for tasks even though they know better. They look at each thing to do, estimate how long each one will take, and then add it up to see how long it will take to meet the deadline. But they usually forget to the time spent dealing with interruptions and emergencies, maybe hoping there won't be any. By the time they realize their mistake, the timeline is looming, increasing their stress.

Although you might not know which specific interruptions or emergencies you'll have to address, you can, based on experience, estimate the average amount of time you will spend in dealing with them. Add your interruption time into the overall time estimate.

TIP 22: IDENTIFY AND ELIMINATE CERTAIN INTERRUPTIONS

You have something to say about a lot of the interruptions you're putting up with, and when and how they happen.

Take control of your availability to others, and re-train people to value your time.

What are the top three kinds of interruptions you deal with every week? We're betting if you look, you'll find a definite, almost predictable pattern of types, or times of day, or both. Maybe your interruptions happen first thing in the morning, right after lunch, or near the end of the day. Maybe it's phone calls, or office drop-ins, or deliveries that command your attention. If you look closely, you may even be able to predict who is going to be the source of the next interruption and what it will be about.

You can reduce recurring interruptions and even eliminate some of them. First, examine how you make them possible. If you maintain an open door policy instead of having scheduled office hours, you can change that practice. If you answer the phone when it rings instead of scheduling times for taking and returning calls, you can change that too. You have trained people to interrupt you, and you can retrain them whenever you choose.

One manager we know removed all the side chairs from his office. He realized he had been encouraging visitors and chat times. To emphasize the change he wanted to make, he got rid of some furniture. Another executive, who was working on deadline for a board presentation, posted a sign on her door that said "Interrupt ONLY for one of these three things [which she listed]. Otherwise please make an appointment to see me during open-office hours." In both of these cases, interruptions decreased. As a side benefit, other people started working harder too. When you commit to productivity it sends a message.

Eliminating some predictable interruptions is one way deadline busters take control of their time, and gain respect for their work schedules.

TIP 23: STAND BY YOUR TEAM

Your team is a whole network of people who
can assist your success in meeting your deadline.
If you want them to give all they have, speak well of them.

The people who contribute to your success deserve your support,
even when they make a mistake.

None of us meets or beats a deadline without the help and assistance of other people. Even though you might not have a staff, or dedicated staff resources to rely on, there is still an extended network of people involved in your success. They might be knowledge resources, gatekeepers to people or systems, or any variety of people who have some relationship to your deadline work. These are the people you want to promote, cultivate, and support. Stand by your team.

What you say to—and about—these people makes a big difference in the velocity of your work. If you gossip or complain about any one of them to anybody, you hurt your own chances of success. Words spoken in the workplace are rarely kept private. Assume that whatever you say is in public view, and that negative things said about people in your network are unhealthy for your projects. Talk about people's strengths and accomplishments and stay silent about negative opinions or unflattering rumors.

If you want people to work hard for you, you need to work hard for them. If you want people to help you meet a deadline, they need to know you're on their side. Help the people on your team when they are in trouble, and go to bat for them whenever you can. When people know you speak up for them, and not against them, they're more willing to go the extra mile for you.

It's hardest to stand by a team member when something goes wrong or is criticized. But when someone on your team makes a decision, stand by that person and treat it as your decision. Accept responsibility and don't embarrass people. This sends a clear signal that they're part of your team even when things get tough. They won't forget it.

TIP 24: INVOLVE OTHERS EARLY

The sooner you can involve key people, the better. If you're not sure when you might need them, or even what you might need them to do, at least show them your plans. Give them an opportunity to be involved.

The people who might be important to your success should be notified well in advance of your needing their time or attention.

Look at everything you will need to meet and beat your deadline, from top to bottom and start to finish. Identify all the people whose assistance you're likely to need for any reason, even if you aren't sure how or when you'll use them. These are the people you want to involve early.

Potential resource people need to know your objectives and understand why you think they might be called upon at some point to give you a hand or an ear. Talk to them to clarify their possible role and the timing of their involvement. Even if you don't use them, they will feel included and appreciate that you gave them a head's-up.

Some people could inhibit your success just because they do not know about your deadline or their possible role in it. They need to see what you're doing in order to provide effective support. The goal is to avoid ever having someone say, "Why didn't you tell me sooner?"

If you've mapped out how you plan to meet your deadline, you know who you need to include in your performance network. You also know when you might need them, and what you might want them to provide. Since everyone has his or her own deadlines to meet, get their attention early in the game. Don't risk that they'll be too busy at a crucial time.

Make sure you take time to go over your work plan with them, and get their input and ideas. Answer any of their questions and agree about whether and when you need to talk again.

TIP 25: EXPAND YOUR RELATIONSHIP WITH PEOPLE

Deadline busters know the quality of their relationship with people can influence whether a deadline is met or not. You can expand the relationship you have with people.

Have you ever noticed that some people never talk to you unless they need something? Or that some people don't give you the whole picture, but just throw you a few crumbs of information now and then? How do you feel about those people? Do you go out of your way to help them, or do you let them fend for themselves?

Most of the results produced in organizations are a direct result of the relationships between people. Where groups or individuals are negatively competitive or secretive, the quality or timeliness of results and communications may be compromised. You're better off sharing information, respecting their input, and keeping them aware of your objectives than playing office power games.

Taking good care of your workplace relationships requires more than just informal networking. Show an authentic interest in other people, listen to their concerns and objectives, and speak positively about the future. You don't have to be great friends with everyone, but you do need other people's assistance if you intend to consistently meet deadlines. Their assistance may ultimately depend on the quality of the relationship.

If you go to people only when you need something, they won't be reliable partners in your success. In most organizations, there are few partners, but lots of people who want something. A partnership is built on shared respect for objectives, and opens the path to cooperation that can make a big difference at the end of the day.

It's worth your investment to create strong partner and ally relationships, unless you want to do everything yourself.

TIP 26: MAKE THEM AN OFFER THEY CAN'T REFUSE

When people hesitate to give you the support you need,
you might have to give them something they want.
Learn what it is and use it as your bargaining chip.

Sometimes you need help from people who are hesitant or reluctant to give it. People often say no when they are working on deadline, and don't see how to make time to honor your request. The reality in most organizations is that people are overloaded and can't take on one more thing. Unless you are someone who can mandate their work and priorities, you'll have to get in line.

When this happens, see if you can make them an offer they can't refuse. Find something you think will be so attractive they'd be foolish to pass it up. For example, you might offer to take on a tricky part of some assignment they have, or connect them to a valued resource, or loan them staff or budget resources to give them a needed boost.

If you know that you need something unreasonable from someone, and you suspect you'll get a no, you might as well look for something that will sweeten the deal. In order to make a good an offer, find out what they want or need. It's not a bad idea to ask them: "What would make the biggest difference in your situation right now? If something would help you out, what would it be?"

Once you know what they want, see if you can find some way to provide it or help them get something that would make a substantial difference to them. If you can, make the offer: "Here's what I need from you, and I'm hoping if I give you this it will help you enough that you'll be able to help me in return." Don't be shy about admitting that you are bargaining for a particular kind of assistance. This isn't something you want to do as an ordinary practice, but when you need it, it's good to know how to make a deal.

TIP 27: MAKE YOUR DEADLINE PUBLIC

Publicity helps you make things happen.
By making your deadline a matter of public conversation,
you give others an opportunity to contribute to its accomplishment.

Public statements also give people notice
to get out of the way and not obstruct your intentions.

Many people keep their deadlines to themselves, or share it only with a small group of those who need to know. They work in a stealth-like manner. It's usually smarter to tell lots of people about the deadline and what is going be involved in accomplishing it. One way to go public is through the use of displays.

One reason we don't go public is we assume other people have their own deadlines and don't want to be bothered with ours. Another reason might be out of self-preservation; if nobody knows about your deadline, they won't know if you fail. So you might not say much more than, "I'm working on this thing for Howard," or "I've got to get this done for the VP."

You could be a lot more out-front than that, as a matter of policy. Keeping things private can work against accomplishing the deadline. The more people who know what your objectives are, the more opportunity they'll have to see ways their work is related to yours. This opens a channel for people to contribute ideas, access to resources, and even the resources themselves.

Yes, you risk telling people who don't care much about it, and you risk having a bigger audience than you may be comfortable with. But you can gain support, and you also reduce problems. By taking your deadline public, people may avoid taking actions that would confound your plans. They can also let you know where some landmines are. Put public conversations to work on your side, with as few secrets as possible.

Going public is a way to "burn the boats". Often, the more talk for accomplishing a deadline, the more likely its success.

TIP 28: LET THEM ALL KNOW WHAT'S HAPPENING

Let people know what's happening with your timeline, your problems and your solutions. Just because you know how things stand doesn't mean other people do.

It makes your life easier to keep everyone in the loop, and to have as big a loop as you can get.

Think of a time when you placed your order in a restaurant and then your waitperson seemingly vanished—no drinks, no food, nothing. Or when you had a medical exam and nobody called you back about the test results. You find yourself waiting and wondering, without a clue as to what is happening.

People get anxious when they don't know—they can worry and wonder whenever they're out of the loop. Some people will worry that something is wrong, or wonder why no one is telling them what's happening. Some people may be afraid to ask.

When people don't have answers, they fill the void with all kinds of thoughts. They make stuff up! Usually whatever they invent is far worse than whatever is happening. Don't let the people working around you live in a mystery. Let them know what's happening. Blab, and give them the latest. Not just some of them—all of them. Let your team know, and your boss, your customers and anyone else you think either is, or should be, interested in the success of the deadline.

Don't tell them just any old thing. Tell them what's been accomplished, which problems have been solved, and what's going to happen in the near future. Don't whine, complain or make excuses—promote your work. If you need something, ask for it. And, of course, if they said they would do something for you, remind them about it.

In real estate, the adage is location, location, location. With deadlines, it's communicate, communicate, communicate. Don't let people wonder about the status of the deadline, the team, or you. End their suspense and let them know. It will make your life easier.

TIP 29: HAVE REGULARLY SCHEDULED, ACTIVE MEETINGS

Stay ahead by looking ahead. Have regular meetings that look at the actions to be taken in the near future and the long-range future.

It's better to cause the future than to be a victim to whatever comes along.

You can tackle a deadline assignment in two ways. You can be reactive, and respond to whatever is happening. Or you can be active, and *cause* things to happen. Active is better, and more fun besides.

An active stance toward meeting a deadline will position you for the future in a powerful way. You'll be engaged in causing or making things happen instead of trying to cope, or deal with events. Looking ahead to see what's next helps everyone recognize all the things that are coming up, decide what to do about them, and agree on the appropriate actions to take. One good way to do this is with scheduled, active meetings.

Active meetings are different than informational meetings, or debriefing (or post-mortem) meetings because they are always looking forward to see whatever needs to be done next. In some cases, what's next is solving a problem or dealing with a breakdown that just happened. In other cases it's simply doing what's next on the master plan or schedule. Whatever it is, What's Next? is the topic of the meeting.

Your meetings are also to review progress toward accomplishing the deadline. This means looking at what worked well and what didn't, reviewing the schedule of work, and determining the most appropriate actions to be taken next, by whom and by when.

The purpose of these meetings is to determine what needs to be done to increase velocity and momentum, then to commit to taking appropriate actions. At subsequent meetings, follow up on all promises made and repeat the process.

Tip 30: Don't Wait, Do Something Now

The normal tendency with deadlines is to wait until later to get started,
but that increases the likelihood of failure plus adds stress.

Do yourself a favor. Do something now.

"Don't just stand there, do something!" We've all heard that from someone who wanted to prod us into taking action now, today.

The normal human response to deadlines is to wait until later to get started. In fact, statistics show people often wait until almost half the time available is gone before getting to work on whatever is due. Remember high school term papers? This kind of postponement is procrastination.

But saying you procrastinate makes it sound like you're idling, as if you have no other deadlines. Most often, though, lots of other things are due—you're always pretty busy, right? That means any *new* deadline you get is far enough into the future that you feel comfortable delaying the start time. You aren't idling, you're working on things that seem more pressing or have a higher priority.

Unfortunately, putting off getting started only makes matters worse and increases the likelihood of missing the deadline. It can also give you that frantic, stressed sense of being behind that comes with looming deadlines.

Sometimes you wait because you think you can't go forward until someone else does something. For example, maybe you're waiting for an authorization to spend money. But in many cases, this waiting is just a pretext for not getting other things going. You usually know about other things you could do, so waiting is your choice, not a mandate.

Deadline busters know that waiting increases the likelihood of failure. Acting today has benefits tomorrow, so it's smart to act, even if only to refine the plan and start identifying and assembling the resources.

TIP 31: PULL, DON'T PUSH THEM FORWARD

Fear can be a powerful motivator in the short term,
but it's not a good long-term strategy.

If you want people to support you over the long term to reach your deadline,
try appealing to the things they consider important.

There is probably no stronger fear in organizations than the fear of failure. The humiliation or embarrassment that comes with looking bad in the eyes of your co-workers is a strong motivational force. Fear can give you the emotional kick you sometimes need to overcome a challenge.

But fear is not a long-term winner. People don't like being afraid or intimidated. Fear pushes people into action. Try pulling people with commitment instead of pushing them with fear.

You can use the future to pull people forward by focusing on their commitments, the commitments of the project you're working on, and the positive aspects of what you're trying to accomplish. This isn't positive thinking, it's paying positive attention to people and work.

Talking about commitment and goals improves the way you relate to the job and the people. We know a manager who says, "People are basically lazy and won't do much unless you stay on them." It's a well-established principle that you get what you expect from people, and he did. Nobody wants to disappoint you.

Most people want to do what's right, and look good in the eyes of their co-workers in the process. People like to succeed, to win, and to know that their participation makes a difference.

Pull people forward by focusing on what they want—success—rather than the failure or punishments they'd rather avoid. Talk about the positives, even the benefits and lessons gained from mistakes and problems. Talk about the difference the end result is going to make for the customer, the user, and the company. Give people something that pulls them into a future that looks good to them, and they'll use their own energy and talent to get there.

TIP 32: USE PUBLIC DISPLAYS

One of the most effective ways of communicating the status of a deadline is with public displays—charts, graphics, signs, etc.
Displays let people see what is happening and how their performance toward the deadline is progressing.

Let people see what needs to be done without having to being told.

How can you let everybody know the progress on a deadline without meeting or talking to them? Use a visual display to keep the status of deadlines up in front of them. Most of you have seen the United Way thermometer—a great example of a visual display.

A display is a visual presentation that shows the current status of a project, and lets everyone see how much territory you've covered and how much farther you have to go. Other examples of displays are: scoreboards at sporting events, dashboards in cars, and flight instruments in airplane cockpits.

Displays allow people to see what you want to accomplish, and just how far you've gotten at this particular time. If you arrive late to the baseball game, you'll know where things stand by looking at the scoreboard.

It's true that a picture is worth a thousand words. The power of displays comes from the fact that they give people a picture of what's going on. They can see it without having to read a report, and it's easy to understand even for people who aren't on the deadline team. Everyone can tell whether things are stalled or racing ahead.

Two conditions must be met for displays to be effective. First, they must be understandable when you look at them. If you make them too complicated, they aren't useful. A common display for a deadline chart is to color green all those the tasks that are successfully on schedule, color yellow those that are pending or in jeopardy, and color red all the overdue ones. A glance shows you the status of the whole game.

The other condition is displays must be updated regularly. If they aren't maintained, people stop relying on them to get the news about deadline status, and the display loses its value. Keep the visual display current.

TIP 33: DEBRIEF, BUT DON'T SECOND-GUESS

Have regular debriefing meetings to have people report on what's happened, review lessons learned, and identify new issues that have surfaced. But don't second-guess what could or should have been done.

Focus on what was done, what can be learned, and how it changes your next actions.

Make it a regular practice to debrief what has happened when your work reaches a milestone. Identify what worked, what didn't, and what to learn from all that. It may be tempting to talk about what might have happened if you'd made different decisions or if things had gone some other way, but it's not a good investment of anyone's time to do that. That's called second-guessing, or twenty-twenty hindsight. Use your debrief meeting to review events without having people get defensive.

A debrief meeting doesn't try to get people to commit to future actions. It's just a time to freely and completely look at the past, say what needs to be said, and share some lessons learned. You want the new insights, ideas, or discoveries that came out of the work that's been done so far. Let everyone involved take a clinical look at what can be learned that will improve future performance.

Have debrief meetings for your successes as well as failures. If you debrief only failures, people may come to see them as punitive and withhold the very information you need. Debriefing successes lets you see why you were successful. Was it luck or brilliance? You might find some actions that can be developed into routines and used again in the future.

Make debriefing a practice that happens for every milestone, no matter what the outcome. Make it clear this is an opportunity for learning and improving, not for second-guessing or should've-could've-if-only. It's a place to tell the truth, be analytical, and incorporate that education into future practices and policies for busting deadlines.

TIP 34: GIVE THEM A CHANCE TO FAIL

Your ability to meet deadlines expands in direct proportion
to the growth of the people working with you.
They will grow both by succeeding and by failing.

Give people a chance to learn, grow, and develop.
Let them make their own mistakes.

A manager once told us, "I learn a hundred times more from the mistakes I make than from what people tell me or try to teach me. When someone tells me something, I might get the idea, but I don't get the experience. When I try something and fail, I understand what works, what doesn't, and why. And I have a real experience I can rely on in the future."

Failure is an excellent teacher if you are willing to learn from it. But sometimes when you are on deadline, you can become so concerned with avoiding failure anywhere in the whole project that you start to micromanage. If you focus on the details of what everyone else is doing in addition to your own tasks, you can cause new problems. You can go over the edge when you start telling people how to do things, instead of just telling them what to do. Exerting more control doesn't always reduce the risk of failure.

Since most people genuinely learn by making their own mistakes, it's useful to give them plenty of room to learn their job. Education and training is great, but you can't rely on your own ability to pay close attention to what many other people are doing. Giving them some latitude will expand their ability to think for themselves, and improve your chances of meeting the deadline.

Instead of telling them what to do, try asking *them* what should be done. After they've done it, have them tell you about the outcomes, good and bad. People can develop the ability to consider a situation, see what is needed, and provide the right stuff. They'll also learn from their mistakes if you practice regular debriefing meetings. If they become dependent on being told what to do, you'll be working harder than you like.

TIP 35: FOCUS ON THE DELIVERABLES

Meeting a deadline means you'll be delivering what is wanted to the people who want it. But, to be successful you also need certain things delivered to you—what you want, when and where you want it. The best way to make that happen is to focus on those deliverables.

Project management tools are great, but if you don't know what the deliverables are, nothing will save you from failure.

You can focus your attention on two different places when you're trying to accomplish a deadline. One place is *how* something is done; you look at all the steps, actions and processes required to get something done. The other place is *what* is produced out of each step or action: you look at the products, services, or communications that need to go from one place or person to another in order to achieve the final outcome. These products, services, and communications are called deliverables, or handoffs because they are delivered from one place to another, or handed off from one group or person to another.

When you focus on deliverables, you pay attention to the quality and characteristics of your project's products, services, and communications. Deliverables are not vague concepts like quality or satisfaction; they always have very specific objective characteristics like timing, quantities, measures, etc. They also have a specific sender and receiver. The sender is the provider, or resource manager. The receiver is the customer, and gets to say if the deliverable meets the desired criteria.

Deadline busters know the key to success rests in focusing on what is to be delivered, not only *by* them, but also *to* them. Identify everything you need from others and get what you need. Invest your energy in being clear on the specifications, requirements, and conditions of the deliveries you make to others, and on what others must deliver to you. Focus on the handoffs and leave processing or production details to whoever is accountable.

Focusing on deliverables requires you to shift your attention from watching what people do to watching the outputs of what they do. If you want to meet deadlines, it is a shift you will want to make.

TIP 36: CREATE A DEADLINE SCOREBOARD

Scoreboards are a way for all the players and all observers to know how the game is going. Scoreboards show statistics on the basics necessary to understanding the progress of the game.

Create scoreboards that show people the status of all key tasks and results required to meet or beat the deadline.

Scoreboards are an integral part of every major sport and every type of game. Without scoreboards, it's impossible for players or spectators to know the status of the game. How many times have you seen a player look up at a scoreboard to check on how things stand? Scoreboards allow players to determine what difference a particular decision or action they took made in the game. The same is true with deadlines. Players and observers like to see movement in the details and specifics of the game.

A deadline scoreboard is a public display that allows anyone and everyone to know immediately the status a deadline or a set of deadlines. Is the project meeting its timeline? Will it make the deadline on schedule? Are things ahead or behind? By how much?

Creating a deadline scoreboard requires you to determine the most useful things for players and observers to see. Get input from others to help you do this. Ask people, "What are the measures we could post and update regularly that will let you *see* what you want to know? Is it the percent of tasks completed? The number of days we're ahead or behind schedule? The list of items to be done this week?

Put your deadline scoreboard in a prominent place so it is visible to remind people how their piece fits into the bigger picture of the deadline. Make sure the scoreboard is updated regularly to keep it fresh and encourage people to refer to it.

Some managers bring their deadline scoreboard to the weekly staff or project meetings. They use it to assist in debriefing and also for exploring what's next. It gets everyone involved in updating the status and it returns them to the ultimate objective: busting the deadline.

TIP 37: DON'T RELY ON TRADITION

People rely on traditional ways of doing things to get most of their work done. But, when it comes to deadlines, we can't rely on traditional methods if they aren't working. At those times, you have to be willing to experiment to find new ways to succeed.

Doing things the way you've always done them is depending on tradition and experience to get things done. Sometimes it works. Lots of things can be done with the kinds of tools and techniques we've used before. But tradition doesn't work for everything. Sometimes you need to break from tradition and try something new.

If things start grinding down or stalling, and the deadline looks farther from your grasp, you need to take new action. In studies of organizational decline, there is a saying that success breeds failure. How is that possible? Because once you find a way to do something that works, you tend to stick with it. But sticking with it can also get you stuck.

People have ways of encouraging you to stay stuck. They'll tell you, "If it's not broken, don't fix it," and, "Don't reinvent the wheel." But sometimes they haven't noticed that it *is* broken, and sometimes you *do* need to invent a new wheel. You can believe in old methods and tools as long as they are producing great results. When that slows or stops, ditch them and get creative.

We once saw a task in a NASA project plan that said, "New metal invented by this date." Now that's bold. When the success of your space flight depends on inventing something that doesn't exist, you are playing for breakthroughs. You can establish a research-and-development mindset for your work, and be on the lookout for sticking points and for new ideas to get unstuck.

If your deadline is already at risk, start experimenting with all your assumptions. Examine your beliefs like crime scene investigators examine the evidence to learn what happened. Then, use your findings to invent new ways to succeed.

Tip 38: Expect the Unexpected

Deadline busters know that when things don't go as expected, unprepared people can respond in unproductive ways. People can train themselves to expect the unexpected. Then, when the unexpected happens, they aren't disabled by the surprise.

The motto of the Boy Scouts is "Be Prepared." Good advice, particularly when you realize that the motto urges them to be prepared for anything, even the things they don't think will happen, or can't imagine would happen. Maybe it's possible to be prepared for the unexpected.

Everyone has expectations about what should happen. When we flip a light switch, we expect the light to turn on. When we press the brake pedal in our car, we expect the car to slow and stop. When we sit on a chair, we expect it to hold us without breaking. If these things don't work the way we expect them to, we are surprised and sometimes upset.

Getting upset is very often the way people respond to unexpected information or events. They can get frustrated, angry, irritated, or agitated, and when they cool down, either try to get things back to normal or figure out why they got caught off guard.

In either case, the response is not productive. You'll always be better off working on realities and dealing with the situation at hand than trying to return to the past. The past is not always an ideal. A past-based response can disable you by blinding you to what's really here in the present.

You can short-circuit the typical, ineffective response to surprises by expecting the unexpected. Build time into your plan for unexpected breakdowns, events, and victories. Don't make a plan so tight it depends on the universe lining up with it—sometimes the universe has a mind of its own. Approach your deadline expecting the unexpected, and when things happen, you'll be open to dealing with the new situation you've got instead of trying to restore the way things were supposed to go.

TIP 39: ANTICIPATE BREAKDOWNS AND FAILURES

If you take the time to plan and schedule the work required to bust your deadline, you'll find places where there is a chance of failure, or where slight variations could cause problems or slowdowns. These are the places to examine for alternative actions to avoid or mitigate potential problems.

Create your contingency plans at the first place in your plan you see something could go amiss.

Murphy's Law says that if anything can go wrong, it will. If you develop the schedule of all the work that needs to be completed in order to accomplish your deadline, you'll notice the places in your plan where Murphy is likely to be right.

You'll see where, for example, you're depending on a supplier who has a history of lateness. Or you may see that you're counting on getting an approval from someone who could be on vacation when you need their input. Or you might see you've only allowed three weeks to finish something that has never been done in less than four.

While it's true that everything might go exactly as you've scheduled it, it's also possible that Murphy will be right. You are better off assuming that some of them might go to Murphy, and change your plan accordingly.

Identify and understand all of the high-risk assumptions that are built into your work plan. Find out where breakdowns and failures are most likely, and which ones could cost you the deadline if they didn't go your way. List all the problems you could encounter based on the schedule, people, and resources you've planned. Then figure out ways to reduce the risk.

What can you do about suppliers to ensure on-time delivery? Can you get approvals earlier, before vacations? Is there a reason to believe some things can be done more quickly now than they were in the past? Once you've studied the risks, you can take action to avoid the pitfalls or reduce the cost of the problems.

Deadline busters know some deadlines are missed because people don't plan for problems, and when they happen they're unprepared to deal with them. You can anticipate failures by examining work plans, find where they might be lurking, and take actions to avoid or reduce the risks or costs.

Tip 40: Maintain a Deadline Inventory

Keep track of every single deadline assignment or agreement.
Keep track of the current status of each one.

A good way to track your deadline assignments is to
create and maintain a deadline inventory.

Take a few minutes right now to list of all the deadlines you have. Not just the big ones, but all of them. Write down every product, service, or communication you owe to someone else, even if you don't yet have a specific due date for it. Now, next to each one, indicate the status: is it unscheduled, ahead of schedule, on time, or late?

If you're like most people who have done this not-so-little exercise, you had to refer to your to-do lists, calendar, and stacks on your desk to remember some of your deadlines. You might have remembered most of them, but when you looked in these other places, you probably found more. Rarely does someone remember every single deadline.

Now, here's the question: If you can't remember your deadlines, how can you expect to meet them? You cannot rely entirely on your memory to know what's due, let alone what needs to be done next. You've got to have a good system for tracking all of your deadline assignments.

One reason people miss deadlines is they forget them. Really—people forget the deadlines until someone or something reminds them, usually when it's too late to do things right and on time. People have a limited amount of short-term memory and it's very easy to overload it and forget things. As a result, something you're sure you could never forget one minute can be completely gone the next. If you're going to meet deadlines, you need something more reliable than memory for keeping track of them.

A deadline inventory is a comprehensive list (electronic or paper) of all your deadlines. It shows you what is to be delivered, to whom, and when. It can also show the status of each, such as green highlight for something on or ahead of schedule, yellow for one in danger of falling behind, and red for anything behind or overdue.

The inventory allows you to keep track of everything you have due. To be effective, it needs to be updated daily.

TIP 41: ANTICIPATE CHALLENGES FROM SUCCESSES TOO

Successes, particularly when they happen early in your timeline, can pose a risk to meeting deadlines. An unplanned success can encourage people to think it will be easy, and kick back a bit.

Don't take the chance of losing momentum. Plan to have some extra deadline-boosting activities ready for times you've had accelerated results.

Most people know failures and breakdowns can blow a deadline, so preparing for them makes sense. But few people realize successes can also blow a deadline. The idea that successes could lead to failure seems nonsensical, but there's a special risk when things go much better than expected. What happens if you get far ahead of your schedule? You kick back, take it a little easier, and enjoy the slack.

That's how success can lead to failure. People become complacent. The success tells them they've figured out what it takes to succeed. So they kick back a little, assuming the remainder of the work will be as easy as what they've already done. When people feel they have spare time, they lose their sense of urgency, and take their foot off the gas.

Like the fable of the race between the tortoise and the hare, when the hare was well ahead of the tortoise he stopped running and settled down for a nap. By the time he woke up, the tortoise was already crossing the finish line.

Just as you plan for breakdowns and problems, plan for what to do if you have a big breakthrough. The momentum of your work is a precious resource, and once you've built some momentum you don't want to lose it. Getting ahead of schedule is an opportunity to add extra value to the products, services, and communications that are the engine for your project. Put people to work on adding that value, or smoothing out hurdles to the future. Keep the momentum growing.

Anticipate successes. Be ready to put people to work on some relevant deadline-boosting activities so when success-surprises happen you're ready to use the extra acceleration it brings you.

Tip 42: Build In Slack, but Be Careful How You Use It

A standard procedure for dealing with uncertainty is to build in slack—extra time in your work plan. But if you build it in, you must be very careful how you use it, or you'll find it's gone when you need it.

Everyone who has managed work for a deadline knows things happen that weren't expected—interruptions, delays, and things that don't work as planned. One way people have learned to deal with these problems is they build slack into their schedules.

Slack is extra time, beyond what you calculate you'll need to meet your deadline. If you know from experience it will take fifteen days to install a new system, you might prefer to promise it will be done in twenty-one days. That gives you six days of slack in case you need to deal with unanticipated problems and unexpected events.

The purpose of slack is to provide time to deal with things that happen outside your control: equipment failures, staffing losses, and other unforeseeable things. Slack time is not intended to be used to give people more time to get things done, but that's often exactly what people do with it: they slow down. When everyone knows slack time is built into the deadline plan, they don't operate with a sense of urgency.

You have two options. One is not to use slack time—none at all. This is hardball. It has you hold people to account for their promises and play full-out to do the work without a cushion.

The other option is to let people know how much slack there is, and let them bargain for its use. The people on your team can work out who gets it, and for what purpose. If you do this, you cannot withhold any emergency slack or you'll lose their trust. You have to make it very clear that this is all there is, there is no more, and when it's gone, it's gone. Keep a tight rein on this one: slack can breed slackness.

TIP 43: TREAT ALL DEADLINES AS HIGH PRIORITY PROMISES

Beware of priorities. People often use one job's priority as an excuse for not doing other things. It can cause people to question your credibility for keeping the promises you make.

Take the point of view that all your promises are high priority, and then operate accordingly.

How many different types of deadlines do you have? Do some deadlines have a higher priority than others? If so, what determines the priority? Is it based on who gave you the assignment, or on the customer's needs, or is it a matter of which people you like better than others? Deadline busters know any time you've said yes to a deadline, you've given your word to something. Your word is always a high priority.

When you hear people talk about priorities, suspect a smokescreen. The smoke can keep you from seeing the promises that won't be kept because priority—a higher order phenomenon than promises—is going to take precedence.

You can choose to operate as if there is no higher priority than your promises to other people. When you make a promise, you promise to deliver a certain thing by a certain time. You've created an agreement with someone else. If you put that promise in the back seat as soon as something called a priority comes along, you might be blowing smoke.

Of course, maybe when you said yes to the delivery and due date, you said, "I'll do it provided no one more important asks me to do something else, or provided nothing more important comes along, in which case, all bets are off." If you said that, it's probably okay to blow off the deadline. They were warned.

People who use priorities do it because they said yes without thinking about the commitment they were making. They said yes, but left the door open for doing no. They also opened the gates to priority-escalation; once you say you missed a deadline because of higher priorities, people will increase the priority of their deadlines to get you to do them.

To keep your integrity in buff condition, however, it's better for you to stay on track with keeping your promises. Deadline busters treat all their promises as high priority.

TIP 44: BE GENEROUS WITH THANKS AND APPRECIATION

You can afford to be generous with thanks and appreciation.
People never seem to get enough of either, so if you are generous with both, it
will set you apart from almost everyone else.

We sometimes think the only way to reward people is with money, promotions, or raises. True, these things are nice. However, the resources for them are limited and may not be under your control. The other thing is they aren't always what people want most.

People don't feel appreciated, recognized for what they are doing now, or known for what they've done in the past. Some feel they've been taken for granted or treated as part of a corporate machine. So it's not surprising people say they want more recognition at work.

Recognition comes in many forms. You may not have dollar resources, but you have absolute and complete control over your appreciation of people's contributions. When you tell people how much you appreciate them for what they have done, and you recognize what they had to give up or deal with in order to get it done, you've given them a very powerful reward. Saying a genuine, authentic "thank you" counts more than you can imagine. A heartfelt recognition is often valued more than more traditional rewards.

Have you ever done your best, or even gone beyond your best, to get something done for someone who never said thanks? Remember how it felt? Thank-you and appreciation are missing in organizations, so when you thank and appreciate people, they notice it. This kind of recognition can have a profound and enduring impact. Think of the last time someone said thanks to you, or told you how much they appreciated what you did for them. How did it make you feel? Would you be willing to do something for them again? Odds are you would.

Give people the gift of your thanks and appreciation, and do it often. It matters.

TIP 45: GIVE THEM WHAT THEY NEED TO SUCCEED

You can be tough about holding people to their promises,
but if you want to develop them as partners in busting deadlines,
you'll have to talk to them about the resources needed
to do the job—and be prepared to help obtain them.

We can ask people to do almost anything, but their ability to deliver depends on whether they have what it takes to accomplish the job. If we expect people to meet deadlines, we need to be sure they:

1. Know the requirements they must satisfy,

2. Have specific due dates by when they are to meet those requirements, and

3. Possess the information, resources, and knowledge necessary to do the job.

People need to know what's expected of them if they are to succeed. The best way to do this is to focus on what they are going to deliver. Telling someone, "I expect you do to a good job" is not as effective as saying, "I want the ABC proposal done in the standard company report format with no grammatical or typographical errors." Then clarify the due date. One advantage to getting this specific is it allows people to think about what resources—information, training, and material—they need to do the job.

Knowing the resources needed is part of understanding the deliverable and the timeline. If people do not understand what resources are needed, they don't know what to ask for, and you can't support their success. When you ask someone to make a promise for a delivery with a due date, you are making an agreement with them. As part of that agreement, you are both responsible for seeing that the necessary resources can be acquired.

Consistently meeting deadlines requires you to help others identify and obtain the resources and training they need to complete the work successfully.

TIP 46: SCHEDULE YOUR DUES AND THEN DO THEM

<u>All</u> the work required to beat the deadline—your work and the work of your team members—needs to go on a calendar.
Then it has to add up to a successful on-time delivery.

Make sure everything gets scheduled in a way that, if everyone did what was in the calendar, the project would be successful.
Then do it as scheduled.

Deadlines are deliveries that have due dates. They usually require several steps, and each step takes time. That means each step, phase, and task has to be scheduled in a way that ensures it will get done. So far, so good. But how do we do that?

The most important job is to think through everything that has to be completed in order to meet the deadline. It might be a giant list, or just a few things. But for every single one of those tasks or events, it's important to spell out how long you think it will take. That's right: estimate the time, and other resources too, for every single activity.

Yes, it does take time to do that, time you could be doing something else. But if you don't, you cannot schedule to win. Everything you do takes some amount of time. It might take a few minutes or it might take many hours spread out over several months. If you itemize the parts of the job, estimate the time each will take, and schedule each one of them in an honest-to-goodness calendar, you have a good idea if and when the promised due dates can be met.

Identify everything you can think of that needs to be done to accomplish the deadline—at least everything you can see at the moment. Estimate the time and resources each one needs to be complete. Block out the times required to do the work in your calendar. Then, as much as you can (remember, unexpected things happen), follow the schedule. Schedule the work, and do the work as scheduled.

Bottom line: when all the to-dos needed to meet the deadline are blocked out in your schedule, you can see when the work will get done. Nothing is more critical to meeting deadlines than this. Deadline busters use and protect their schedules.

TIP 47: KNOW WHAT ELSE PEOPLE ARE WORKING ON

Meeting deadlines depends on the availability of other people, but sometimes people say they're available when they're not.

Know what else they are working on so you can determine your confidence level in their promise to you.

The people who do some of the tasks and activities to help you meet your deadlines are valuable resources. They also have other things to do. It's a good bet those people are doing, or have promised to do, other things for other people. In today's organizations, everyone is busy. Most people say they have more to do than time to do it, so you can't assume anyone is a dedicated resource, even when you think they should be. Still, if they're helping you, you can consider them to be on your team.

It pays to know what the people on your team are working on, no matter whether they report to you or someone else. That way you know how available they are. People tend to be optimistic about their ability to get things done, and often commit to more than they can deliver. Once you realize they're overcommitted, it may be too late to salvage your deadline.

While this kind of over-promising and under-delivering is always a problem, it's particularly distressing when you're working on deadline. Don't fall victim to someone else's availability. Find out what people are working on, and what types of deadlines they have at the moment. Get to know what they have stacked up in front of them.

This lets you know something about the type of demands they need to juggle, and will give you more—or less—confidence in their promises to produce results as you need them.

You rely on people to be available, so you'll want to make sure their yes is reliable. If you suspect it isn't, allow extra time to compensate for their optimism, or find an alternative way to get it done. Handle this now rather than wait until later when you'll have less time to adjust the resources.

TIP 48: CELEBRATE WITH EVERYONE

Michael Jordan was arguably the greatest basketball player who ever played the game. But even when he made the basket that won the NBA championship, he celebrated the victory with his teammates.

Anyone who has played on a team knows that some people get more attention than others, but it takes the team to produce the win.

Celebrate the victory with everyone so they know that you know they contributed.

Everyone likes to win, and most people like to celebrate victories. People want to participate in the jubilation that comes with success or completion, especially when the work was difficult. Give people the opportunity to celebrate victories, large and small, and invite everyone, not just the stars.

Meeting a deadline is a team affair. Even when it looks as if one person did most of the work, other people gave time, energy, money, etc. to meet the deadline. When you do beat the deadline, remember to include all the people who contributed directly or indirectly in at least some of the recognitions and celebrations you have.

You don't have to have big celebrations; pizza parties work just fine. But your celebrations do have to be in honor of the victory. Find a way to display something that reminds people of the deadline they busted so everyone knows it's not just a party—it's a victory party. Be sure you and other people say something about what was accomplished.

Some people will say, "I didn't really do anything." Involve them anyway, and let them know you valued what they did and you know it contributed to the final score. Give everyone a chance to see that what they did was considered important by you and others.

Sometimes you need to go beyond this to invite the unseen and the unheard supporters: the spouses and families who provided background support. If the project required their patience, understanding and personal involvement—late evenings at the office and weekend work, for example—they've earned this kind of exceptional recognition. Without their contribution, the team wouldn't have been able to win.

They may not make it to the celebration, but they won't forget the invitation.

TIP 49: PAY ATTENTION TO THE THINGS YOU DO WANT

One behavioral principle says you'll get more of whatever you reward. Since a premium reward for people is getting your attention, it's good to be careful what kind of things you give your attention to.

Don't pay attention to the things you don't want more of. Identify what you do want, and then give those things your attention and recognition.

What happens when people do a good job in supporting you to meet your deadline? Do you praise them for doing what they said they would do? Do you notice them when they give you on-time performance? Or do you treat their good work as if they're just their doing their job, and not requiring special recognition?

People like to know when they've done something well, and they want a little attention for it. If you pay attention only to the problems and miscommunications, you run the risk of getting more of them! Some people will do anything for a little attention, even if it means getting scolded.

In the absence of positive feedback, many people working with you will not assume they are doing a good job. They may not know their work is valuable to your deadline success. In fact, they may assume just the opposite; many people tend to de-value their worth to others. It's worth your attention to discover and acknowledge the actions people take that help you reach your goals.

This technique also works to improve some of the specific types of skills you want people on your team to have. For example, if you want people to be accountable, notice someone who was accountable for something and call attention to it. If you want people to improve their on-time performance, find someone who got their work in on-time and let everyone know about that.

Paying attention to the behaviors and results you want to see more often is a form of recognizing desirable behavior. When you learn who is doing things the way you want them done, you can encourage it by giving it your attention. Elaborate incentive systems aren't always necessary.

TIP 50: DEVELOP AND USE ROUTINES AND CHECKLISTS

Many things we do are routine. Pilots, for example, routinely prepare the plane for takeoff. But, because their routine is a life and death matter, they use a checklist.

If there are tasks you need to do over and over, it's easy to forget something, especially if the task is complex or has many parts.
It's worth your time to define it as a routine—create the checklist to be sure it's done properly.

Some tasks need to be done in a particular way, either because that's the most efficient way, or because it's required by regulations or by downstream users. The best way to ensure that recurring tasks are done right is to define them as a specific routine. That means taking the time to spell out the specifics. What needs to be done? What are the acceptable ranges of results? What needs to happen if something is outside the range? Then, just like an airplane pilot who reviews everything before each takeoff and landing, the process can be easily replicated by other people.

To make performing the routine easier and smarter, develop a checklist for every step, every action, and every result that needs to be completed. Include notes on what to do with the various outcomes at each step. This kind of checklist can be used to improve a recurring process and also to train people to do it for you. That's what lets a pilot go through the same routine regardless of his flight experience, the plane he is flying, or the weather at the destination city.

Without checklists, you can forget things or respond to critical situations in inappropriate or ineffective ways. If you doubt this, ask the people on your team, "What would you do if the customer asked for a change in the specs? Or, "What procedures should you follow in an emergency?" Their answers will tell you if you need a checklist.

Mail order companies use packing lists to verify that everything ordered is being shipped. Meeting managers use agendas to remember to cover everything important. Routine checklists can be designed to remove the variability that produces mistakes and inconsistencies in certain processes. Deadline busters know routines and checklists are time savers and the time investment to create them is worth it.

TIP 51: INTERROGATE EXCUSES AND EXPLANATIONS

Beware of buying excuses: everyone is too busy, understaffed, waiting for something, etc. When you settle for an explanation of poor results, you're missing a chance to help people produce better ones.

Build accountability by going beyond the excuses and explanations that are designed to transfer blame.

It's normal for people to give excuses and explanations for why something went wrong. If you listen, you'll notice that excuses and explanations usually shift responsibility away from the excuse-maker and say someone or something else is at fault.

It may be hard to tell which excuses are valid, and should be accepted, versus the ones just serving as a disguise. It's difficult because there really *are* many factors involved in any disappointing outcome or outright failure. But there isn't much power in settling for that explanation. If we don't look deeper to see what could have been done to avoid or reduce the problems, we won't learn how to improve things for the next deadline.

In this light, any excuse could be valid, but almost no excuse is going to give you the total source of a failure. It's more useful to look at all the sources you can think of, and all the things that people could have said, done, or decided that would have helped produce a better outcome.

You get to the source of a delivery failure by interrogating the excuse. Ask the questions to learn all of the decisions and actions that were taken, by whom, and when and how. If you debrief long enough you'll see what alternative decisions or actions would have produced a better result.

When someone is late for your meeting and tells you it's because of traffic, or another meeting that ran overtime, or an unexpected phone call, do you buy it? When someone doesn't deliver a product on time, blaming a system crash, changes in specs or some other emergency, do you buy it? Or do you dig deeper to find the underlying points where a different decision or action would have given a different, more satisfying outcome?

Things go wrong for a lot of reasons, and if we let things slide with a good excuse, we keep those reasons hidden. Interrogating excuses reveals the reasons along with better alternatives. It also builds accountability at the same time it reduces excuse-giving.

TIP 52: REWARD THE SMALL WINS

A proverb says even a journey of a thousand miles begins with a single step.
Few deadlines are completed in one giant step—they are an accumulation of
many small tasks done by many different people.
If you want people to continue to perform throughout a long journey, reward
the small wins along the way.

No deadline is beaten all at once, in some single heroic accomplishment. Most deadlines are accomplished through the accumulation of many small successes, many of which require ordinary work by ordinary people. If those small steps are not taken, or not completed when required, the entire deadline could be compromised.

Waiting until the final deadline before recognizing people for their contribution will probably mean that many people, and many small actions that made a difference, will be forgotten. It's hard to remember the things people did weeks and months ago, even when they were important to the accomplishment of the deadline. At the end, many things and people may be overlooked. Some of those who are overlooked may be resentful, or disappointed they've been taken for granted.

You can avoid all that if you reward the small wins. When you give attention and recognition to the intermediate tasks and accomplishments, it allows people to see their work in a new light. Their contribution is recognized and appreciated. Acknowledging small wins helps to build a momentum for success.

To do this successfully, of course, you need to have clear criteria for showing progress and wins along the way. Short-term milestones are useful, and so is having a hero of the week award or some similar opportunity to nominate those ordinary tasks that made a big difference to others.

It is much easier to build and sustain momentum by rewarding a series of small wins on a long journey than to re-energize when things start to fade. Recognize small wins on the way to the bigger, more distant, reward.

TIP 53: PACE YOURSELF

Pacing the work not only reduces the need to rush, but also assures ample time for dealing with unexpected issues that might arise.

Marathon runners know the key to running a successful race is pacing oneself. If they run too fast, they'll tire and be unable to finish strong. If they run too slowly, they fall behind too far to be able to make up the distance at the end. Unfortunately, most people ignore the principle of pacing themselves when they work toward a deadline.

The way most people deal with a deadline is by starting slow and increasing the amount of work they do as the due date gets closer until, at the end, they are working frantically to get everything done. Sometimes, because they haven't scheduled the work to set a productive pace, people try to do things on the fly, improvising as they go.

Sound familiar? If a marathon runner starts slow, and tries to make up the distance in a sprint, they may find the stress is too great to allow them to finish the race. At work, when people are in a hurry there will be stress, and more mistakes, and less time to correct the problems that arise.

The best way to pace your work for meeting a deadline is to schedule the necessary tasks, and make sure you pace it for a uniform or even pattern. No snail-crawling and no sprints. The proper pace will be supported by clearly identified delivery milestones and intermediate deadlines at regular intervals.

Setting a good pace will reduce the stress and pressure of having to hurry up as deadlines approach. When your work is paced evenly over the whole timeline, the quality is higher and so is the consistency in meeting deadlines.

Deadline busters know that being rushed to finish is a major threat to any deadline. So they pace themselves.

TIP 54: ASK FOR WHAT YOU WANT, AS A DELIVERABLE

One reason deadlines are missed is that people misunderstand what you're asking for. These misunderstandings cost time, and they also cause resentments that undermine the accomplishment of subsequent deadlines. This problem can be avoided when you specify what you want as a deliverable.

If you need something to accomplish a deadline, how do you ask for it? Do you ask for things in general, non-specific terms, like, "I need more resources," or, "I need clearer specifications," or, "I need better support from our vendors." If so, what might be clear to you isn't necessarily clear to the person you're asking. In fact, it might sound like a vague complaint instead of a request you want then to satisfy. This lack of clarity creates misunderstandings that can be expensive when trying to meet a deadline.

A good way to increase clarity and eliminate misunderstandings is to focus on deliverables. Then, when you need something, you can ask for it as a deliverable. In the examples above, asking for resources, clearer specifications or better support is simply too vague. What is the deliverable? What product, service, or communication will satisfy the need?

Asking for deliverables requires you to get specific about exactly what you want delivered to you. If you want more resources, be prepared to say how much and in what form. Would an increase in spending authorization work, or would simply being free to spend existing funds without prior authorization work? When you can specify what options will work for you, it's easier to ask for—and get—what you need.

One reason deadlines are missed is that people misunderstand what you want. Then they give you whatever *they* think you need. When you take the time to know what you need and ask others for a specific deliverable, you make it easier for people to give you the right thing. Deadline busters know the time spent to ask for the deliverable helps everyone win.

TIP 55: IF YOU'RE GOING TO PANIC, PANIC EARLY

Although panic can be detrimental, it's also a powerful motivator of action. Therefore, if you are going to panic, do it early so it gets everyone into action while you still have time to correct any mistakes.

If panicking gets you into action and helps you get things moving, it can be an effective tool instead of a problem or a distraction. Unless, that is, you are close to the due date. Panic at that time is just frenzy, and causes stress and mistakes for yourself and for the people around you. As you get closer to the due date, panicking becomes more and more dysfunctional, and it's best to avoid it.

In the normal conduct of working to meet or beat a deadline, people tend to panic late in the game. Some people get very anxious, worried, concerned, etc. as the due date draws closer. The proximity of the deadline increases urgency and, for some, a sense of impending doom.

When a deadline seems far off, most of us feel we have plenty of time and don't have much sense of urgency. If we panic at this early stage, we will probably hear something like, "Calm down. What are you all worked up about? We have plenty of time." But what if it was okay to panic early? What if we could do it in a way that has other people in action instead of trying to calm us down?

One way to panic early and effectively is by giving people immediate assignments with specific due dates and time. Using short deadlines early in the project gives people a sense of urgency and gets things moving at a good pace.

Another way to panic early is to get your outside resource people involved early. Ask for their advice, insights and recommendations. The sooner you talk it up about what's required to meet the deadline, the better your chances of avoiding the late-panic rush.

TIP 56: LEARN TO SAY NO WITH AUTHORITY

Anyone can say no. But few people can say no without sounding as if they are complaining or resisting. Can you say no with authority?

One way to put yourself in a position of speaking with authority is to schedule all the work you are going to do. Then you can accept or decline requests based on your availability. If you're already booked, you'll have to say no—with authority.

One of the smallest words in the English language is no. Still, it may be one of the most difficult words to say. If you are going to tell the truth about what you can and cannot do, no is one of the words you'll need to use.

What does it mean to say no with authority? It means that when you say no, or when you counter-offer a request, you do so with authoritative knowledge. You have a complete understanding of the work you've already committed to do, and a reasonable estimation of the time it will take to deliver it.

You've done your homework. You are an authority on your schedule. You know when you are—and are not—available and you can communicate that availability with certainty. You know where and when you must say no. If necessary, you can even show someone your schedule of times you've committed for tasks and events as the basis for your no.

Anyone can say yes. In fact, one of the reasons deadlines are missed is that people say yes to things they can't deliver. They accept requests without having a schedule of their already committed work. The result is that some work goes undone, requiring excuses. People rarely admit to not scheduling their work. Saying yes and doing no is a deadline buster's no-no.

What it takes to be able to say no with authority is doing the up-front work on your schedule. If you think through your work and schedule the time to do it so you can meet your deadlines, you have the authority to say no. You are in a much more powerful position than simply saying "No, I have too much to do" or, "No, there's not enough time" without having done the work to know if its true. A thoughtful schedule is a deadline buster's best friend.

TIP 57: CREATE A CLIMATE OF NO COMPLAINTS

The climate in which people work will influence the way they work on deadlines. If the climate is supportive and positive, people tend to be positive and supportive. One of the best ways to build a positive climate is to discourage uncommitted complaints.

Have you ever been in a good mood and walked into a meeting where people were complaining about things? What happened to your mood? Did it come down, at least a little? Did you find yourself joining in the complaining? Complaints invite more complaints, and left unchecked, they can turn a positive environment sour.

A complaint is not a fact. A complaint is a whine—it's a comment about what's wrong with a person, an organization, a policy—it lacks a commitment to getting the complaint resolved. It's a way of talking that pretends to be positive ("Someone should stop those guys from cutting corners on the contract"), but it's really blaming other people—someone—for not solving a problem.

Complaining without a commitment to causing a solution is an energy sapper. If you go into any group that has poor morale, you'll find a culture of complaining. Sometimes people even complain about poor morale! Complaining reinforces a sense of powerlessness—"There's nothing I can do"—in the workplace. It drains away productivity, participation, and enthusiasm.

You can reduce and eventually eliminate workplace complaining. Make a new policy: Complain only to someone who is in a position to do something about it. Then instruct everyone to redirect each complaint to whichever person or group can most likely resolve it. Interrupt people who are complaining to you about something you can't fix, and send them to the people who can take effective action regarding the issue. If they won't go, don't let them complain to you about it any more. If there's no one who can resolve the issue, ask that the topic be dropped. With no solution in the future, complaining just wears people down and misuses their energy.

This is hardball, but it works. Make it your policy to support people in upgrading their complaints to include some commitment to getting it resolved. Don't complain and don't let others do it either. Deadline busters don't entertain complaints they can't handle.

TIP 58: FOCUS ON THE SOLUTIONS, NOT ONLY ON THE PROBLEMS

When you meet with the people on your team, or people assisting or supporting your deadline project, what do you talk about?
Do you talk about problems, breakdowns and troubles?
Or do you discuss actions to move things forward?

All progress is a function of what you talk about. If you want to meet and beat deadlines, identify the problems and talk about the solutions.

The CIO for a large hospital system had a "go live" deadline for a new information system to complete an integration with a recently acquired local hospital. Unfortunately, the conversion project was already several weeks behind schedule, and looked as if it might continue falling further behind each week.

At the executive staff meetings, the CIO's team leaders detailed the problems they were having in the conversion process. Each one presented a lengthy laundry list of problems, with detailed discussions of some of them. Some completed their reports with a recommendation to study one or more specific problems in light of new information.

Troubled by the lack of progress, the CIO reviewed the meeting notes and recommendations, looking for a way to turn things around. She saw that her meetings were focused on finding and discussing problems, and decided to change the meeting agenda. She asked her team leaders to recommend at least one solution to every problem they reported. She wanted to hear the problems, but she also wanted people to think about what might resolve them. Within six weeks the velocity of the project improved, and at thirteen weeks was almost entirely back on schedule.

It takes action to make something happen. Investigating and discussing problems *seems* like taking action, but in fact nothing is moving until something is implemented. When people start talking about solutions, they can move into action by implementing their ideas. Identify problems, but don't dwell on them. Shift the focus to dwelling on solutions. Deadline busters use this tip to pick up velocity on a complex project.

TIP 59: GET PEOPLE INTO ACTION—MAKE REQUESTS

People need to understand things in order to know what to do. But under-standing alone is rarely sufficient to get them to do it. The only thing that gets people into action is to make a request. For best results, combine explanations with your requests.

Have you ever been in a meeting where everyone around the table understood and agreed with the actions proposed, then left the meeting and didn't take the actions? Or, have you ever given a thorough explanation of what to do and the importance of doing it, then had people nod their heads, say, "I understand", then still not do it? Parents recognize this impasse, and so do most managers.

One reason action doesn't automatically follow explanation and understand-ing is that understanding does not cause action. People understand how to lose weight—diet and exercise—right? But understanding does not cause action. Requests cause action. You explained it, but you forgot to ask if they would do it!

When you make a specific request, "Will you do this?" that requires someone to say, "Yes, I'll do that," or, "No, I won't do that," you've created action. You will either have their promise to do it, or you will know you need to look else-where for action.

We usually don't make requests because we don't think we should have to ask them if they will do it. We think, "They see what needs to be done, and they know it's their job, so they will do it." Not necessarily, and if they do, well it might not be on your timetable.

Requests get people into action. When you ask someone to take an action or produce a result by some specific time, you have a much better chance of causing an action than if you trust understanding alone. If you want action, make requests.

Of course, explanations are useful but remember to add a request. After explaining a new technique, you can say something like, "I want you to do it the way I explained. Will you do that by tomorrow?" The request makes it clear what you want and when. Their response commits them to action.

TIP 60: LET THEM KNOW WHAT YOU'RE DOING

It can be upsetting to people when someone they work with starts doing things differently without explaining why. Let people know you are working on improving your ability to meet and beat deadlines and that you'll be doing some things in different ways. They may not like it, but at least they will understand why.

Have you ever had a friend who suddenly started doing things differently without any explanation for the change? Maybe she went on a diet or quit smoking. Maybe she attended a leadership or management seminar and came back doing things you had never seen her do before. Or maybe she met someone and is now head over heels in love and doesn't join the usual conversations any more. It's as if the old person you knew has been replaced by someone else who now acts in new ways.

We are creatures of habit and the people around us have learned our habits. They have learned what we do, when we do it, and how we are likely to react to things. In a sense, we've trained them in how we operate, just as they have trained us in what to expect from them.

When we change any of our habitual ways of doing things, it disrupts communications and relationships. What was predictable and known is no longer reliable. People can't count on us to do things we did before, which means they may also have to change what *they* do.

Not knowing why we have changed adds to the problem. If you change something, they want to know why. People want to know what happened, and if you don't tell them, they will make up their own explanations, which may not be very accurate or flattering to you.

Tell people what you are doing and give them some reasons for it. Tell them you are working to improve your ability to meet deadlines. Let them know you'll be trying some new things because you want to be more successful. Tell them you'd like their support. It only takes one person who is willing to consistently talk about meeting deadlines to get others interested. Let people know what you are up to and give them the chance to participate with you.

TIP 61: TALK ABOUT WHAT WILL BE—NOT WHAT ISN'T YET

People frequently talk about what isn't done and how much is left to do. This type of talk can be overdone, and ultimately very de-motivating, because it's about losing, not winning.

Busting a deadline is assisted by focusing on winning. To do this, ask people to say to what will things be like when it's done rather than talk about what isn't done.

Our relationship to the work we have to do can be seen in the way we talk about it. One way people talk about their work is from a deficit perspective: "I have too much to do," "I'm way behind," "I have no time,", "This isn't done yet," "I need more help," etc. It's as if they're trying to climb out of a deep hole that keeps getting deeper. Even when you point out the progress they've made, they say, "But I still have all this other stuff to do." Some people live with the burden of what isn't done, and no matter what they accomplish it's never enough to reduce the deficit.

If you're honest, you know there will *always* be a deficit. Even if you finish everything on your list today, there will be another list tomorrow. That's life: there are things to be done.

Deficit talk is a tiring and defeatist conversation. Deficit talk is disempowering and de-motivating because it's about failure, loss, and being behind with no way of ever getting ahead.

You can take the initiative to have people say something new if you can get them talking about the results and benefits of their work. You can ask, "When this part is done, what will we be able to do?" or, "When these things are finished, what percent of the project will be complete?" or, "When that is taken care of, how will it benefit the user?" Take the time to develop this conversation. It's not always easy because you're talking about a future that doesn't exist yet. But it gets you out of purely deficit talk.

Instead of talking about what isn't (the deficit), talk about what will be (the gain). This might seem like a semantic trick, but it does cause a shift in perspective from seeing a burden to seeing a positive future. When people think about what will be gained by their work, it can give them a new context and a new perspective for what they do.

TIP 62: WHEN TROUBLE COMES, ASK FOR HELP

If you run into trouble with meeting your deadline, or you're concerned you aren't going to make a key milestone, you may want to keep your head down and work harder. Don't do it. The go-it-alone habit can work against your success.

When you run into trouble, don't clam up—ask for help. Talk about your authentic concerns, and get input—ideas and other resources—from other people who can help you. Don't be a Lone Ranger.

Most of us will do almost anything to avoid looking bad in front of others, particularly if they are important to our careers. We want people to believe we are capable, competent, and in control.

Is it any surprise that when we run into trouble we have a tendency to keep it to ourselves? Many of us have the habit of pretending everything is fine, though it should be pointed out this is more likely among men than women. We assume that if we just keep quiet we can turn things around and no damage will have been done. It's a version of the adage "What they don't know won't hurt them."

The difficulty is that when things go wrong, there is a need for more communication, not less. It takes a big person to admit that they are having trouble and that things are not going as planned or expected. It takes a person who is more committed to meeting the deadline than to how they look. When things go wrong, more conversations, ideas and discussions are needed, not fewer.

You don't need to tell everyone everything. When you encounter problems, you want to involve the best people available in solving them. Gossiping or complaining about the problem to your co-workers doesn't help resolve the problem and it might make it worse. You want to take your issue to the people who are in a position to help resolve it. In some cases these people are on your team and it's just a matter of having a straightforward conversation with them about where things stand. In other cases, it might mean going to your boss or other resource people and asking for assistance.

It can be disconcerting to admit you are having trouble with something you consider important. But it's much better to ask for help when you need it than to risk missing the deadline. People will learn that you'll do what is needed to meet a deadline, including asking for help.

TIP 63: KEEP TRACK OF WHAT PEOPLE OWE YOU

Every time someone says "I'll do that" to help you meet your deadline, take it seriously. Consider they now owe you something. Keep track of that promise as you would track any other debt: what do they owe you and when will they deliver? You'll need a reliable tracking system that makes all the promised resources visible to everyone.

Let people know their promise is important to you. Let them know you keep track of what they say they will do. This helps build people's accountability, and it also increases your ability to meet deadlines.

The successful accomplishment of any deadline requires people to do the things they said they would do, and do them when they said they would. But how do you keep track of what everyone says they'll do? How do you track their promises so you know what to expect and when to expect it?

You need a system that will let you see what has been promised by everybody, along with the timeline for each promise. You probably know your memory is not highly reliable. It only takes a few "I forgots" to create problems. And, when it comes to deadlines, forgetting can be catastrophic.

Some deadline busters keep a log of Things Owed, or a chart of Promises Due, in which they specify three things: what is owed, who owes it, and when it's due. This three-column list makes it possible for you to regularly review everything that is due to you, your deadline, and your team.

Having this tracking tool is important because it lets you know what you can expect from others. It is equally important that you let people know you have this tool and that you use it. This tells people you take their promises seriously, and they know their promised contribution is an important part of your success.

When you say to someone, "Let's have lunch," and they pull out their calendar, you know they are taking the lunch idea seriously. Similarly, you want people to know you're adding their promise to your list. At the bottom of holding someone to account is being able to track whatever you expect them to deliver. A good tracking tool helps you build accountability.

TIP 64: GET OVER IT, CLEAN IT UP, AND MOVE ON

When something doesn't go as you wanted it to go, don't brood too long. Talk to the appropriate parties, clean up misunderstandings or broken agreements and move on. Just as carrying too much baggage on a trip can slow you down, holding grudges can be tiring too. Rather than go forward with that kind of burden, get in communication with people, repair broken agreements, and move ahead.

When something doesn't go the way you expected, or someone drops the ball and doesn't deliver what they promised, it's natural to get upset, angry, or frustrated. These are all normal responses to things going wrong. But when these responses linger or grow into resentments or regrets, they can displace clear thinking and effective action.

Have you ever known someone who was talking about something as if it happened recently, but it actually happened weeks, months or even years ago? The person might have lost a promotion or a job, or been blind-sided by a customer or vendor, and they are still talking about it with all the emotion of the original event. Sometimes they add more bitterness to the injustice of the now-historical event every time they tell the tale.

When something goes wrong, you can dwell on it or you can get over it, clean it up, and move on. Getting over it requires you to be as honest as possible about the situation and own up to the facts. The next step is to accept the way things are now and quit fussing over the way things might have been if things had happened differently.

Whatever happened, it gives you a new reality. It's time to look at the situation as it exists now—you might as well stop arguing and wondering about it. If you can see what's in front of you as just an unplanned reality, you've effectively gotten over it.

Sometimes, getting over it includes clearing things up with another person or group. You may have to change some agreements, deal with some consequences of broken agreements and soothe some ruffled feathers. The alternative—resentment, grudges and making people pay—is a bad use of your time and energy, and undermines any future relationship with people you might need.

Once you've gotten over it and cleaned things up, the next step is to move on: do the work needed now, in today's reality.

TIP 65: MAKE IT MATTER

A basic learning principle is that behavior is shaped by its consequences. For this reason, it's useful to establish consequences for meeting or missing your deadline.

When you meet or beat the deadline, what happens? Is there a party to celebrate the victory? Do people get a raise or some recognition? What is the prize for winning?

If you blow the deadline, what happens? Does anyone get fired, transferred or assigned less enjoyable work? Do they miss out on a bonus or a celebration? What is the cost of losing?

If there is no known incentive or benefit for busting a deadline and no penalty for blowing it, people will conclude it doesn't matter much. With no consequences, there's little reason for people to change their behavior or go out of their way.

One of your jobs will be to make the accomplishment of a deadline matter to people. Obviously, that doesn't mean you need to redo the reward and compensation system of the organization. But you do need to get people involved in clarifying or creating the rewards and penalties for meeting or missing the deadline. This helps the consequences belong to everyone, not just to you.

Both the severity and the certainty of consequences are needed to influence behavior. Don't promise a reward you can't give, or threaten something you aren't prepared to deliver.

And remember a few other suggestions in creating consequences:

1. In general, incentives work better than penalties alone.

2. The greater the reward for success, the more likely you'll be successful.

3. The more severe the sanction, the more likely you'll be successful.

Ultimately, you can make your deadline matter to everyone.

TIP 66: COMMUNICATE BREAKDOWNS IMMEDIATELY

When something happens that wasn't supposed to happen, tell the appropriate people immediately. Don't wait to see if it all works out, don't assume they already know, and don't think it is someone else's job to deliver the news. If it's a problem, learn who else it affects and tell them immediately.

Breakdowns, problems and miscommunications are a normal part of meeting deadlines. In fact, it's rare to have a time-constrained job where nothing goes wrong along the way. But all too often, we neglect to communicate these problems to the other people who might be affected by them.

The deadline manager who adopts a wait and see or a self-help approach may be harming a colleague's success. One manager who encountered a computer billing error concentrated on fixing the problem within his own team and failed to notify the accounting department. The result was the people in accounting didn't discover the problem until after the annual report went out. Their numbers were wrong, they were embarrassed, and they were angry that the manager hadn't told them right away.

You don't want to be seen as the boy who cried wolf, crying out every time something doesn't work. Not every problem needs to be communicated to everyone. But take a moment to consider that any problem you encounter might materially affect others. If something causes a delay for you, even a small one, it might be relevant to others in your organization. Look up from your project at the bigger network of players to see if this affects them. If it does, let them know.

When you give people a heads-up that something has happened, and that your deadline or some part of it is at risk, they have the opportunity to prepare contingency plans if they haven't already done so. Don't put other people in the position of having to say "Why didn't you tell me this sooner when I could have done something about it?" These are the same folks from whom you might need a heads-up someplace down the road.

TIP 67: GIVE THEM PROBLEMS, NOT SOLUTIONS

When we're up against the clock, most of us have a tendency to tell other people what to do and how to do it. In other words, we've got a problem, we've already figured out the solution, and now we want someone to perform the solution for us. This can work in a pinch, but most people would prefer to be assigned a problem to solve, and have the opportunity to implement their own solution.

When you were a child, did you like being told what to do? Your parents, teachers and preachers all gave you their solutions for you to implement: clean your room, do your homework, be honest. Most children don't like it, and many adults don't either. In fact, sometimes we don't do it just to show them. Lots of us are still kids when it comes to being told what to do. We would much rather be asked.

One powerful way of asking people to do something is to give them a problem to solve. Many people would rather figure something out than follow instructions. Many people enjoy fixing things, solving problems, and making something broken work again. When you ask them to solve a problem, they are free to create a solution, even though they are still bound to the parameters of the problem.

Gordon Bethune, the CEO of Continental Airlines, used this technique in transforming Continental from the worst airline in the industry to the best in only a few years. He discovered that since the people who were closest to the problem usually knew most about it, they were in the best position to solve it. When you allow these people to create the solutions, they become highly motivated.

When we give people instructions we are also giving them answers or solutions. Ultimately we are training people to depend on us, and they may not develop the ability to think for themselves. This lowers their initiative and increases our own work.

Train people to develop their own solutions. Give them a problem to solve and then provide them with support, coaching, and guidance as needed. But avoid solving the problem for them.

TIP 68: LEAVE THEM ALONE

When you give individuals an assignment, leave them alone to get it done. It's fine to have a schedule for progress reports or updates. But don't interfere in the way they are doing things, and don't keep giving directions as they proceed. Nobody needs to hear, "This is the way to do that" unless it's absolutely necessary.

When you give someone a problem to solve, be sure you also give them the room to solve the problem. Don't be a backseat driver, telling them how to solve it, what to do or how to do it. Don't even tell them what you would do. The idea is for them to learn how to generate the solution(s), instead of relying on you.

Leaving someone alone doesn't mean you abandon them to sink or swim. You'll provide advice and coaching when asked, and keep their attention on the attributes of the solution you're looking for. Ask them questions to have them see for themselves what could be done. For example, if someone is having trouble getting a response from a vendor, you might ask, "What have you done to get the response?", "What have you seen other people do?", "What would be the most outrageous thing you could do to get a response?", or "If your daughter's (son's) life depended on you getting a response, what would you do?" None of these questions tell the person how to get the response they want, but they may trigger some ideas.

You can develop other people's ability to be reliable performers in the future by setting up a schedule for when they'll get back to you with a progress report. Knowing they need to report their results will keep them focused on the objective. And the reports will let you know if you need to step in and give further direction.

Give people the room to show what they can and will do. It shows you are willing to invest in them, and trust their ability to grow into what is needed. Don't hang over their shoulders, or second-guess their ideas. Leave them alone to meet their objectives.

TIP 69: ALWAYS GIVE AND GET SPECIFIC DUE DATES

When you ask people to do things, make sure you include a by-when. When people promise to do things for you, make sure they give you a by-when. An assignment without a due date and time is not an assignment. It is a wish. If the due date you request doesn't work for both of you, negotiate one that does.

Ideally, the deadline you are working on has a specific due date and time. But all the intermediate things that need to be done to accomplish it also need to have due dates and times. That includes tasks you have to do and the ones others are doing for you need to have due dates too.

When you don't give people specific times for turning in results, you set yourself up for failure. People use due dates as a basis for scheduling their work. For example, think of all those unscheduled tasks you have, the things you think you should do someday, but never put on your calendar. There is no urgency, no planning and no coordination without a due date. People postpone work that has no due date, which can increase the likelihood you'll miss your deadline.

Whenever someone else asks you to do something for them, make sure you promise to deliver at a specific date and time. If they don't seem to care, ask them, "Is there a particular time you want or need this? Is there a time you plan to use it?" Don't make an agreement to deliver without a due date.

Research and experience show that both timeliness and quality of performance are better when people are given deadlines by other people than when they establish their own. In other words, people are less likely to meet the deadlines they set for themselves. It's always better for everyone's productivity if you can establish agreed-upon deadlines.

Don't set yourself and others up for disappointments and failure. Always give and get specific due dates.

TIP 70: IT'S READY, AIM, FIRE

Many people have a tendency to act first and think later. Perhaps you have heard people say "I don't have time to plan. I have too much to do." When it comes to deadline busting, you need to do some planning before you jump into action. Although it might look like wasting time while you are doing it, the fact is that planning and preparing for the accomplishment of a deadline are key to making it happen.

"Let's get going. All this talk is a waste of time. We can figure it out as we go." Have you ever heard someone say this when they're asked to come up with a plan? It's a common response when people have pressing deadlines. But the tendency to shoot first and ask questions later can cause real problems.

It is known that planning increases the likelihood of success and it makes doing and managing the work easier too. In spite of this fact, most people don't plan their work. They jump in, relying on their ability to improvise on the run. For many people, planning looks like a waste of time because it seems as if nothing is getting done.

Planning is hard. In part, it's hard because you can't know what will happen in the future. But that is the point. Planning requires you to think about what you want to have happen and what will make it turn out well. That thinking allows you to consider the best sequence of tasks, which resources will be needed at various times, and what agreements should be in place to support a successful outcome. It also requires that you think about possible problems and shortfalls, and what might be done to avoid them, or how to handle them if they do happen. All this gives you a framework for dealing with the unknown future.

A plan is a roadmap for moving forward. Once in place, a plan provides a basis for making decisions and a structure for thinking. It can always be modified and updated to serve as a dynamic tool. A plan is never cast in stone.

Don't shoot wildly. Know your target and how you'll hit it before you fire. You'll find planning gets easier with practice, and helps you hit the target more consistently.

TIP 71: ASK FOR AND GET A WORK SCHEDULE FROM OTHERS

Your ability to meet and beat deadlines often depends on other people producing results for you. Knowing that people are usually pretty bad at scheduling the work they have agreed to do, you want to raise your requirements for accepting their promises. Where possible, get a work schedule from them so you can have more confidence in their promises.

If you manage other people, you need to know if they can produce the results they say they will produce. Although people will tell you, "No problem, it will be done," that doesn't mean it will be. And if you're on the hook for the final result, you need to find potential problem areas before they become real delays, so that you still have time to do something about them.

Most people underestimate the time it takes to get something done and also the number of problems they'll have doing it. Further, most people don't set aside time in their schedules for <u>all</u> the work that needs to be done. As a result, they are overly optimistic about what they can produce in a day or a week. When you're on deadline you can't afford to rely on their optimism. You need to know they have a schedule of their work for your project, and that it accounts for the other things they are working on too.

Perhaps the best way to determine whether people are in a position to deliver what they promise is to place a greater emphasis on their personal work schedules. One deadline buster says, "I have my team bring their calendars to every meeting, and insist they adequately account for all the work that needs to be done." This manager is increasing his own confidence that his people will consider all their tasks and promises, large and small, when making a promise to deliver something new.

If people can't give you a work schedule, or show places in their calendar where the work will get done, you can't rely on their promises. Producing a result takes time and if it isn't scheduled, it's not likely to get produced. By insisting that people maintain integrity in their personal work schedules, you can have more confidence in their promises to deliver.

TIP 72: HONOR THEIR COMMITMENTS TO YOU AND TO OTHERS

Meeting deadlines depends on people doing what they say. When people think it's important to do what they say, it increases the consistency of meeting deadlines. Let everyone on your team know you expect them to do what they say they'll do. One way to do that is to support them in keeping their promises to others.

If you want people to keep their promises to you, be sure to support them in keeping their promises to others as well. Don't undermine their agreements with other co-workers, their families, or anyone else. The manager who tells team members to put the project ahead of other promises is saying, "I don't care what you told them," or "They are just going to have to wait." This is short-sighted.

When we undermine people's promises to others, we also undermine them in keeping their promises to us. They learn they don't have to do what they said as long as they have a good excuse. In the world of deadlines, we count on people doing what they say. Ultimately, no matter what else we might do or say, it comes down to relying on people's word. If they get it in their minds that talk is cheap, the game is lost before it begins. There is simply no accountability possible if people can easily get out of doing what they say by giving excuses or pleading loss of memory.

Interact with people as if what they say to you and to others is important, and let them know it. If they have promises to other people, and you want to displace those promises, you'll need to support them in dealing with the consequences. They may have to clean up any problems caused by the change in plans. Don't let people blame you for breaking their promises to someone else. Don't be someone's excuse.

It doesn't serve anyone to let people off the hook regarding what they have promised. Promises are meant to be kept, and when they are broken there are consequences. Help people be accountable and reliable, not just to you but everywhere in their lives. Let them know their promises matter and you expect them to deliver, renegotiate, or clean up messes accordingly.

TIP 73: PROMISE A RETURN IN EXCHANGE FOR MORE RESOURCES

At times additional resources are needed to meet a deadline. It may be necessary to ask for more money, people, or equipment than you budgeted. A good way to do this is to identify some additional benefits, beyond meeting the deadline, that will result from getting those extra resources. Then promise those benefits and deliver them.

When you need more resources than you expected in order to meet a deadline, how do you get them? What do you tell a manager who is already drowning in requests for more resources that you need more too? How can you make *your* request for additional resources stand out from all the others? One way is to promise a return on the investment.

Some deadlines come with blank checks for getting them done, but not many. Although your goal should be to plan the resources for your deadlines and stick to your budget, at times extra resources are needed. Unexpected mechanical problems, vendor bankruptcy, illness, etc. can hammer your plan. When that happens, more resources may be needed.

Resource controllers have to make tradeoffs, giving resources to some and not others. Usually everyone is asking for more, making those tradeoff decisions difficult. You can threaten that the deadline will be missed if you don't get the resources. That might work, but it burns up good will when you threaten to fail.

Make your request for additional resources more acceptable by stating the benefit—the return on investment—that the organization will get for giving you the resources. More than just meeting the deadline, promise additional benefits to help justify the additional resources. Will this project develop a new organizational capability that can be applied elsewhere? Can costs be lowered somewhere? Will other groups benefit? Get specific: what, who, how much? Identify the benefits, promise to make them happen and follow through.

Promising a good return makes it easier for the resource controllers to give you the additional resources you request.

TIP 74: ACCEPT THEIR DEFINITION OF THE DEADLINE

Misunderstandings can arise when organizations have different types of deadlines. If your organization has firm vs. soft deadlines, or manager vs. staff deadlines, make sure everyone understands what type your deadline is. If there is any disagreement, accept the other person's definition of the deadline and operate accordingly.

Many organizations have different types of deadlines. For example, there are hard deadlines, firm deadlines, soft deadlines, and real deadlines. There are also deadlines for the Board of Directors, CEOs, or Departments, and these may have different urgencies. Some people also have high priority deadlines, or big money deadlines (for high revenue customers). You probably have different types of deadlines in your organization.

When all deadlines are *not* treated as high priority promises, people need some way of determining what they should be working on, and what to do when a new request comes to them. Which tasks should be bumped if a more important one comes in? The point in having these different types of deadlines is so that people can prioritize the things they have due, and schedule their work accordingly.

Disagreement about the type of deadline can cause confusion and missed due dates. For example, everyone might know that deadlines for the CEO take precedence over everything else. But when the chief legal counsel wants something done, she may believe her request has a higher priority than one for the CEO, and expect people to put other things aside. She needs to double-check, because her assumption could be costly.

If you have a deadline, you might see it as "hard" because you have a real due date and can't afford a delay. Your peers on the other hand, might see your deadline as "soft", no matter what you say because they are working on something for the CEO that has no wiggle room in the plan. To be safe, and to preserve the integrity of your deadline schedule, you should assume everyone will treat your deadline from their own perspective. It's your job to learn what that is.

If there are different deadlines in your organization, get clear on what they are, what kind yours is, and then accept that definition. Don't waste time trying to change people's minds about it.

TIP 75: SWEAT THE SMALL STUFF

You've heard the expression, "Don't sweat the small stuff". It's a good reminder to put things in perspective and not worry about unimportant things. But if you want consistently to meet or beat deadlines, those small things are often early warnings and they are important. If you dismiss them without investigation, you may invite bigger problems later when you don't have time to deal with them properly.

The old expression, "Don't sweat the small stuff" is intended to help us put things in perspective and not worry when we don't need to. But if you have a deadline, there is no small stuff. It's all important. When it comes to deadline busting, small problems or glitches need your attention: you should sweat the small stuff.

It seems like a small thing when a team member is late for a phone call, or misses a meeting. It's easy to think it doesn't mean anything and maybe even to make an excuse for them: they've been sick, or have a new baby at home. But small things have a way of snowballing into big things. If you say nothing about it, you're contributing to a more relaxed view of the job. The small things are the harbinger of bigger things to come, as Benjamin Franklin points out:

> *"For the want of a nail, the shoe was lost; for the want of a shoe the horse was lost; and for the want of a horse the rider was lost, being overtaken and slain by the enemy, all for the want of care about a horseshoe nail."*

Sweating the small stuff doesn't mean you should micro-manage. It means you need to stay alert to things that seem out of place, out of character, or strange. It means watch for things that don't seem to fit, or are unusual. It means look for indicators of potential problems and act immediately when you find them.

If someone who is normally on time to work shows up late, find out why. It's out of character and may indicate something is off. If someone doesn't keep an agreement with you or someone else, find out why. You don't want people to think its okay not to keep promises. Besides, it shows you're paying attention and that you care.

TIP 76: HONOR THE SCHEDULE

A poster says "Gravity: It's not just a good idea. It's the law". The same could be said for the schedule of work to accomplish a deadline. A schedule is not simply a good idea, it's the path to accomplishment and the center of gravity for a goal.

Your schedule should be visible and treated as the roadmap to success. Changes should be made when needed, but not without appropriate consideration. Don't allow slippage to pass unrecognized.

Schedules allow us to see what needs to be done and when in order to meet a deadline. Schedules are the only places where all the work required for your deadline can be seen from beginning to end. For this reason, the schedule is a powerful tool for meeting a deadline. But it is a powerful tool only if it is recognized as important.

Make your schedule visible. Put it where everyone can see the timing of things and the inter-dependency of tasks. You don't have to use high-tech software: a simple diagram or table will do. Let people see what will be affected if things don't happen on time. Displaying the schedule provides a way for people to see how their tasks fit into the big picture and consider the consequence their failures might have.

Adhere to the schedule. Have it be the center of your meeting agendas. Relate all assignments and questions to the schedule. If you need to alter or update the schedule, do it as a group, or be sure everyone knows about the change. Then follow the schedule. Do things according to the schedule.

The power of your schedule comes from working to follow it, not from assuming you can always change it. Make changes reluctantly. If you make changes easily, people think the schedule is elastic, and will bargain for extensions. Honor the schedule by holding people to account for their due dates.

You can treat any and all slippage in a schedule, no matter how small at the moment you see it, as a matter of real concern. Don't make a habit of moving things downstream to other time slots, or making it up later. Small variations early on can become very expensive variations later, when you have less time available for dealing with them.

TIP 77: TREAT THE MEASURES AS IF THEY'RE TRUE

Treat your measures as if they are telling you the hard facts about your work performance. Anything less will compromise your ability to meet and beat deadlines.

In his bestselling book "Good to Great," Jim Collins points out that what differentiates great leaders from good leaders is their ability to face facts without denial or rose-colored interpretation. The same is true for deadline busters. There's a difference between what we hope, want or need to happen, and what is in fact happening.

People fool themselves when they design excuses into their measures. Take the deadline buster's favorite measure: per cent of task due dates met. It's a clean scoreboard: picture a list of tasks, each with a due date and a space for writing the actual date completed. It is easy to see when a task is done on time, and to calculate "percent task due dates met". But we are on the slippery slope to failure when we start thinking it's okay to *not* count some missed deadlines because of a special circumstance.

One project manager explained, "It doesn't count if the vendor didn't deliver the supplies we needed." Denial does not alter reality; it only postpones dealing with it.

"Our membership is declining," one association membership manager said, "but not as much as other associations in our same size and type. So we're okay."

No, you're not okay. Your measures tell you something important, and you can listen without trying to insulate yourself from bad news. Don't explain away or deny the statistics. They are reality's feedback to you. If you have measures and data that are valid and up to date, treat them as the truth and make sure others do too. If you don't have good measures, you can get them. Don't rely on feeling good about your project. Get statistical feedback and treat it like gold.

Busting a deadline requires telling the truth about where you are and where you are not. It depends on taking the appropriate action at the appropriate time. Respect the facts of the matter, no matter what they are or how you feel about them. Respect the measured results of your work.

TIP 78: REPAIR BROKEN AGREEMENTS

Any time people don't do what they said they would do, we can say there is a broken agreement. Broken agreements need to be recognized and repaired, otherwise they can contribute to building resentment and lead to a loss of trust and credibility. Make it a policy to find and repair all broken agreements immediately.

Deadlines are rarely accomplished in exactly the way and time they are planned. Sometimes promises are broken—people say they'll do something, and then don't do it. Technically, these occasions are called broken agreements. It's a harsh term, but useful too.

Talking about deadline busting in terms of promises and agreements raises the rigor and seriousness of working to a deadline. It also lets everyone see the way things really get done: by making and honoring requests, promises, and agreements. If you treat uncommunicated absences, late deliveries, and undelivered promises as if they're broken agreements, you set a tone that brings helpful attention to your work from every level.

If you pay attention to every broken agreement, you can use the 5 steps to clean up each and every one of them. If you do this, you will restore velocity to your work. Here are the five steps to repair broken agreements:

1. Admit an agreement is broken, for example, "I said this would be done today, but it won't be ready until Friday."

2. Say why you think it is broken and what will prevent that in the future. "I thought my associate would be able to make the revisions, but he's not here this week. From now on I'll check the vacation calendar before I commit to a due date."

3. Apologize.

4. Acknowledge any costs or consequences as you see them and ask what can be done to moderate them. "I know my missing this due date sets back your project. If you need me to move something else forward, I will get staffing for it today."

5. Make any new agreements needed to clean the slate, such as putting the new due date on the calendar, agreeing to do extra work, or canceling other work.

Although any single broken agreement might not seem like much, the costs can accumulate over time. Repair broken agreements—it's a great investment in meeting and beating your deadline.

TIP 79: RESOLVE PERSONAL CONFLICTS IMMEDIATELY

Anytime people are under stress, which can happen when working under a deadline, they are more likely to say or do things that can cause trouble or upset others. In short, there may be conflicts over what to do that can interfere with delivering on-time quality work. When this happens, insist the people involved resolve their dissention. Don't let conflicts fester or they'll undermine the deadline as well as the productive atmosphere of the workplace.

Personal conflicts and differences arise between people even in the best of circumstances. So it's not surprising they are even more likely when people are working against the time and performance constraints of deadlines. People under pressure can be tense, frustrated or irritable; they may become touchy, and their patience can wear thin. Sometimes tempers can fly and things are said that leave egos bruised and feelings hurt.

One strategy for dealing with these conflicts is to just let things cool off and go away. This is generally not an effective strategy, because is doesn't really clear the air. People who are brooding or pouting over an insult or injury, real or imagined, will complain to others, perhaps sowing dissent and undermining cooperation by having them take sides and make judgments. The longer it persists, the harder it is for people to clean it up, save face, and move on.

A more effective strategy is to insist that personal conflicts must be handled in an adult way: an apology on both sides, an agreement not to gossip and inflame the situation, and a re-commitment to put the workplace values first. You can communicate this publicly, in private one-on-ones, or in small group meetings as the situation requires.

Whatever the method, the people involved need to understand four things: One, the conflict is a potential distraction or disturbance that affects other people and the work they are doing. Two, you expect them to resolve their differences for the sake of the people in workplace and the work obligations of the group. Three, you know they are adults and can do this. Four, you genuinely appreciate their willingness to honor their commitments to larger goals above their temporary but inflammatory excitements.

When even minor differences arise, don't wait. Heated disagreement reflects passion and commitment—useful energy, as long as it doesn't become dysfunctional.

TIP 80: STOP FLYING BLIND: REPORT RESULTS REGULARLY

There is a danger in flying blind: you can't tell where you are or where you're going, and without this knowledge, you can't make course corrections. Keep people up to speed by reporting results and status regularly. All those involved in accomplishing the deadline should see what is and isn't working, so they can make the necessary adjustments.

One thing people say they like about bowling is the immediate visual feedback. They can see how well they did as soon as the ball gets to the end of the alley. Imagine draping a curtain across the alley. The ball would still go to the pins, and you could still hear that something happened, but you wouldn't be able to see the result. You would be bowling blind.

If you don't know what results you're producing, you are unable to improve your performance by making adjustments in your timing, style, or behaviors. At best, you can make an educated guess based on your personal experience and environmental cues, but it would only be a guess. You would have no way to know if any changes you made produced the desired effect.

For many people in an organization, meeting a deadline is like bowling blind. They do their jobs as they know them, and then wonder what happened. They might hear some noise and conclude what they did was okay, but they don't know for sure. As a result, they have no way of correcting or improving the results the next time around.

Pilots know something about flying blind when bad weather prevents visual feedback. That's why they learn to fly by instruments. The instrument reports tell them their flight status and what corrections need to be made to arrive safely and on time.

Knowing your results is of little value if you don't communicate that knowledge to all the people engaged in producing those results. People do not like flying blind. Remove the curtain and allow them to see what's happening. Report status and results on a regular basis.

TIP 81: ESTABLISH AGREEMENTS FOR COMMUNICATION AND FOLLOW-UP

Establish agreements to clarify the information that needs to move between people and groups. It will keep the work moving more steadily and offer opportunities for improvements too.

People usually understand they have job responsibilities for their actions and results. But they often overlook the importance of having agreements about *when* to communicate, *what* to communicate, and *to whom* they should communicate. Poor communication is a prime complaint in organizations, and it is due to a lack of knowledge about those specifics.

Surprisingly, people often don't know exactly what they are expected to communicate. How many times have you heard, "Why didn't you tell me?" or, "I didn't know I was supposed to do that"? Breakdowns in communication are a problem any time, but are particularly damaging to meeting a deadline.

You can avoid or at least reduce the problem by developing more specifics about what needs to be communicated, by whom, when, and how. You don't need to detail every single communication, but you can create the routines for being in communication. Do you want reports every day, week or month? Do you prefer written reports, emails, phone messages, or meetings? What do you and other people need to know? Do you want to know only about problems, or do you want to see the status of specific measurable results? Should people notify someone when they complete a task?

Ask yourself:

1. What am I unwilling to be in the dark about, and for how long?

2. What do I need to know in order to do my job effectively?

Putting structures in place to support communications will help keep things moving. Unless people know what to communicate and when, they will not communicate anything or they'll try to guess what is wanted and then do the best they can, which might not be good enough.

TIP 82: DESIGN YOUR MEETINGS

One of the biggest complaints about meetings is that they are a waste of time. Although they can be invaluable to coordinate action, meetings can be ineffective if they are not designed to move things forward. Design your meetings, don't leave them to chance. Create an agenda to manage what people talk about. When you manage what people talk about, you manage the results they produce.

Meetings are essential to accomplish most deadlines. Whether people meet to update schedules, report results, debrief successes and failures, or commit to future actions and results, sitting down together to talk about the deadline work can give you leverage to gain momentum. To be effective, a meeting needs a framework for the ways people will conduct themselves.

A meeting designed to increase momentum or produce results has certain ground rules. People know how to come prepared—what they need to bring, and what they should be prepared to talk about. They also know the meeting is not simply an opportunity to talk about any old thing. The meeting has a clearly stated purpose and an agenda of topics or presentations that will support them in achieving the purpose. Everyone should leave the meeting knowing what has been accomplished and what actions to take next.

You can design your meetings to be productive. Let people know in advance what you want to accomplish out of the meeting, including any specific outcomes. Tell them what decisions need to be made. Make sure everyone who is presenting information is notified well in advance, and put their names on the agenda. Don't rely on people remembering what to bring or having the right information at their fingertips. If the meeting is to review and update the schedule, remind them to bring their calendars and be prepared to recommend changes or discuss concerns about rescheduling. Distribute the agenda, along with any special reminders or instructions, prior to the meeting if possible.

Stick to your agenda and timeline and discourage talk that does not move the conversation toward the results you want to produce. People will learn how your meetings work, they will come prepared, and you can have a productive discussion.

TIP 83: LET THEM TALK IT OUT

If you have the option to either ask people what they think should be done or tell them what to do, opt for asking. People are far more committed to their answers than they are to yours.

When time is on the line, many of us become more directive. That means we are more likely to tell others what to do and how to do it than we are to ask what they think should be done or how they plan to go about it. The rationale for being more directive is that it keeps things going and saves time. Unfortunately, it's more likely to kill off the very discussions that allow people to see what is needed and to understand how they might proceed.

You can let people test their thinking by letting them dive into a discussion and thrash out ideas about the project. It's helpful to let people talk things out, persuade each other, and challenge accepted wisdom. They may need to debate what will and will not work, and what is or is not important. This helps people develop their critical thinking and explore alternatives not otherwise considered.

You may need to bite your tongue, especially when you hear discussion that could be resolved by your own experience and insight. You may think you can get there faster by giving them the answer, but if people haven't gotten their own thinking up to speed about the issue, your time-saving device can backfire. If you undermine people's opportunity to question and explain, they'll miss the chance to articulate their thinking for the benefit of others. But more importantly, you could also suppress their willingness to participate and contribute. If that happens, they'll wait to be told and do nothing more than directed.

There is some risk that people will not be able to work things out for themselves. But if you keep to your deadline schedule, and intervene only if they ask, they'll grow to be valuable partners. And, in case of emergency, you can always tell them what to do.

TIP 84: PUT THE WORK YOU'RE GOING TO DO IN YOUR PERSONAL CALENDAR

Office calendars are great, but having two calendars suggests that some of your commitments are more important than others. They're not. Give yourself one whole life and one whole calendar.

Everything you do to accomplish your deadline will have to be done in some period of time, maybe an hour, maybe over several days or longer. If you estimate the size of those tasks, specifying how long each one will take, you can schedule them. They'll go on a calendar, right?

Which calendar? If you have a big calendar on the office wall, that's fine. If you have a project room where you use project management software and Gantt charts and Pert charts to track the time and resources for each step, that's fine too. But what about your personal calendar? Are your deadline tasks and events in there too?

Many people keep two calendars, one for work commitments and one for personal commitments. But being a deadline buster is about taking your work personally. You have a work life and a personal life, but it's all one life.

Your promises at work are as important as your promises everywhere else. If you say you'll have the sales report done on Friday, you mark off time in your calendar to do it. If you have a dinner date Friday evening, you mark off that time in your calendar too. It's the same calendar because it's the same life.

Of course, you may not have all of your work schedule details in your personal calendar. You don't need to carry that Pert chart on your dinner date. But the idea is to have your deadline work reflected in your personal schedule in a way that lets you see everything you've committed to deliver. That way you won't schedule something over top of something else, and you can have your whole life be important.

Everything you schedule is a personal commitment. Put all your commitments in your personal schedule.

TIP 85: DON'T CRY WOLF: FOLLOW THROUGH

Its great to have people do things for you, but not if they don't finish them and report back to you to close the loop. People learn what matters to you by noticing whether or not you follow through on things.

You remember the story of the shepherd boy who cried wolf. It turns out the boy got so much enjoyment out of watching all the villagers run to his aid whenever he cried, "Wolf!" that he continued to do it even when there was no wolf around. Eventually the villagers stopped responding to his calls. Then, when a wolf did come, no one responded and the wolf feasted.

Saying you need something is like crying wolf. If you need it, people are glad to help. If you don't need it, and you're making up work for people to do, they'll stop producing for you. They'll think you're crying wolf when you give them an assignment.

So, how do people know if you need something or not? Because if you need it, you'll follow through. If you tell people you need something and never check back with them about it, they'll assume you didn't need it in the first place.

Some people will naturally finish the task and report back to you on the results. Other people won't—they may be poor schedulers, or don't know that their promise to do a job includes their responsibility to close the loop with you at the end. Unfortunately, this situation puts the responsibility on you to follow through on whatever you asked them to do. You'll have to check back with some of the people who are doing the work, or they'll think you didn't need it in the first place.

People notice if there's no follow-through, because everyone in today's organizations has too much to do and not enough time. Even the people you think aren't doing much will tell you how overloaded they are. That's why most people develop a way to prioritize what work needs to be done. One way they do that is by noticing who follows through.

Don't ask for things you don't need, and remember who you've assigned to do the tasks. If you ask someone to do something, notice whether—and when—they deliver the result and the follow through report. Follow through with the ones who let it drop. If you're willing to do that, people will realize that when you ask for something, you aren't crying wolf.

5

Being a Star

"Waiting is a trap. There will always be reasons to wait…The truth is, there are only two things in life, reasons, and results, and reasons simply don't count."

—Robert Anthony

Stardom. Most of us are looking to succeed in some way that will make us proud of ourselves and earn the respect of other people. If you have come this far, you are clearly interested in being a star performer. You also probably have a few other characteristics that boost you toward stardom:

1. You know it takes more than sincerity and good intentions to earn a reputation for being reliable; you know it takes consistent action and straight communication;

2. People trust you to tell the truth about what you will and will not do;

3. Your family, friends, and colleagues know they can count on you for timely, high quality responses and results;

4. You manage yourself and others around you to take new ground in whatever game is being played; and

5. You are willing to change the ways you habitually do things and develop new practices and habits to help win the game.

Being a deadline buster takes all these characteristics and translates them into new habits of communication and relationship.

We know everyone in life has deadlines, but we don't all treat them in quite the same way. Still, there is no escape. We have deadlines at work, at home, for social events like dinner out with friends, and for our volunteer and charity work.

121

Whether we meet our deadlines in any of those areas will influence what people say about us and what doors they will open for us in the future.

Being a deadline buster is also about taking charge of your reputation. You don't have much to say about a lot of things in our lives: who your parents are, where you grew up, or which life lessons you've had to learn the hard way. Until now, you may not have known you had anything to say about your reputation. But you do. You can alter the way people see you and the opportunities that can come your way. The choice is yours: you can take your promises seriously, or you can take them casually.

When you honor what you promise, and people know you stand behind your words, they can trust you and have confidence in you. You can become known as a competent and reliable person. It has been our experience that people like that are highly valued and highly respected in organizations of all kinds. And they are well rewarded.

It has also been our experience that, although everyone can be a deadline buster, not everyone will do it. If you pursue being a deadline buster, you're moving beyond the ordinary ways of doing business and conducting your personal life. In fact, it can be said that you are extraordinary.

BEYOND THE ORDINARY

Developing yourself to be a deadline buster is an extraordinary step for anyone to take. Why? Three reasons:

1. First, not everyone understands there is a difference between reasons and results. In ordinary life, people treat reasons and results as interchangeable commodities, and missing deadlines is just business as usual. If I promise to pay you $200 on Wednesday, and then when Wednesday comes I give you a good excuse instead of the money, you can see the difference between the result and the reason. But all our workplace conversations aren't spelled out to look that clear-cut, and many managers are willing to accept the reasons without insisting on the results. It takes an extraordinary person to recognize the two are not the same and they cannot be interchanged without personal and professional consequences.

2. Second, not all people believe they can or should own their work as if it is their personal responsibility. Many people believe their reasons are

true, believe that trying hard is good enough, and feel it's not their fault if the results don't happen. Passively accepting assignments is commonplace, and it takes a rare courage to take the bigger step and honor your workplace promises as if they were your own. When people choose to be responsible for what they promise, they have moved beyond the ordinary into a realm of making things happen rather than just hoping for the best.

3. Finally, not everyone is willing to break the habits of normal office talk and change the way they communicate. Many people talk about meeting deadlines but haven't learned how to listen and speak about responsibility in a way that engages other people powerfully. Building a new skill takes practice, persistence and a willingness to make mistakes. When you take on practicing any of the eighty-five tips for Deadline Busting, you are developing a new form of communication and will begin to see evidence of extraordinary workplace relationships.

MOVING FORWARD

As much as we would like to be able to say, "Congratulations, you can now sit back and wait for stardom," that's not how these ideas work. Nothing happens until you start practicing the tips. We recommend you start today. And here are three tips on how to begin using the eighty-five tips!

Practice One Tip at a Time

Being a star performer doesn't mean you'll reach stardom in a single step. It takes time to alter any of your habits, and then a little more time after that for your reputation to shift. But it doesn't take forever. The land-speed record was set by one manager who reported that within one hour of practicing Tip #46: Schedule Your Dues and Then Do Them, he discovered a new ability to focus:

> "I am much more aware of how I am spending my time now. Scheduling all my tasks almost has a built-in discipline that keeps me focused on the right project to be accomplished at the right time." Dave R.

While we were working on this book, Warren, one of the managers testing the tips, chose just one tip—#2: Make Counteroffers When Necessary—to see what would happen in his office. At the time, Warren said he didn't believe any of the deadlines used in his workplace could be changed, so he planned to test his own belief by trying this one tip.

He was amazed to discover that most deadlines are negotiable. As a result, Warren started making counteroffers to almost every request that people made of him, whether he needed to do it or not. He now says he's gained a new control over his schedule, and at the same time gained confidence that he could get his work done when he promised it would be done. Warren's on-time performance increased dramatically, and everyone around him has noticed that he's working differently, and more effectively, as well as being more responsible in all his communications.

Warren is not the only one to have discovered the power of Tip #2. Here's what another manager told us shortly after implementing the same tip:

> "Deadlines are negotiable! My new favorite question to ask when someone gives me a deadline is, "What would the outcome be if you received what you need on _____ (alternate date) instead of _____ (requested date)?" So far, with the two requests that arrived this morning, this question has interrupted the requestors' patterns and made them stop and think about what they really needed and when they needed it. Most of our business communications seem to be done on autopilot, where people expect a certain answer to whatever they ask for. Negotiating a deadline really interrupts those patterns and brings the interaction to a conscious level." Elaine M.

Pick one tip, something that interests or challenges you, and start practicing that one. Give it a week so you can test it in a variety of situations and with different people. Then pick another one to test next week.

Building new habits take time. It's easier to develop a new habit if you do it in small doses rather than all at once. Some of these tips take a little more time to master than others, so try testing one at a time. That way you can practice with each one to get it customized so that it fits into your life and your other work habits.

Invite Others to Join You

Marty, the CEO of a federal credit union, tells us he picks out one tip before each of his staff meetings, then discusses it with his staff. He wants his staff people to think about how a particular tip might be applied in their own jobs and how it might improve performance in the credit union as a whole.

Even if you aren't a CEO, you can do something similar with the people who work with you. Take one tip, tell people about it and ask what they think about the idea of using it. Ask them:

- Would it be practical for us to try this in our workplace?
- What effects would it have on communications?
- How would it affect the work or the schedule?

You could even suggest they test it and practice the tip for a day or a week, then follow up and learn how it worked for the people who used it.

Just as with exercise or any other kind of learning, it's generally more fun when you do things with other people instead of by yourself. In the case of Deadline Busting, you are going to learn more if you have other people working on practicing some of the tips along with you.

But, if no one else wants to play, don't let that stop you. You can still practice the tips by yourself. It's okay that not everyone wants to be a deadline buster. Trust your judgment, and if you think practicing a tip will benefit you and your workplace, you're probably right. So do it!

Use Deadline Busting as a Reference Book

Anita, one of the managers who helped us develop this book, says she uses Deadline Busting as a constant reference for new ideas, meeting topics and plans for what to do next in developing her staff. "Once is not enough when it comes to reading the tips," Anita tells us.

Managers who worked on this book found every time they read the tips, they saw something new they could do, or gained a deeper understanding of the whole idea of deadline busting and the difference it can make in their organizations. Few of us can read something once and then master it in practice. So keep the book handy, refer to it often, and steer yourself and your organization to new levels of performance success.

Practicing Stardom

Stardom is not an event. Being a star performer is an ongoing practice of sharpening your skills and breaking through your own boundaries. As you practice these tips, you'll be changing the way you operate at work and in other arenas too. People will notice a positive difference in you, and will begin to relate to you in new ways. We've seen the results so often that we are confident you will be reaping the benefits in traditional ways (money, recognition, and reputation) as well as some unexpected ways too.

In fact, let us know how your Deadline Busting practice is coming along: contact us via our website www.deadlinebusting.com. We just might quote *you* in the next book!

About the Authors

Jeffrey Ford, Ph.D. (organizational behavior) and Laurie Ford, Ph.D. (engineering) are partners in Critical Path Consultants, with consulting, programs, and writing that focus on issues of workplace performance and change management. Jeffrey is also associate professor of management in the Max M. Fisher College of Business at The Ohio State University.

Jeffrey's background in organizational design and change has led to the development of a conversational approach to both general management and change management. As a professional educator, he uses the principles of these methods in designing programs to help people make new things happen in organizations. Laurie's background as an engineer provides her the powerful tools of operations research and network theory. She has developed the framework for a unique "hotwiring" method that locates the sources of organizational performance problems, and designs and implements the most practical solutions.

This husband/wife team combines backgrounds in theory and practice to help people in organizations bring new and fast-acting changes to the performance issues they care about. These solutions appear in their "The Great Managing Ezine"[1], a twice-monthly electronic newsletter for executives and managers.

---

1.   The Great Managing Ezine can be found at http://www.deadlinebusting.com

Index

978-0-595-33906-
0-595-33906-9

Made in the USA
Middletown, DE
23 April 2015